The Modernisation of Russia 1856–1985

John Laver

Series Editors
Martin Collier
Rosemary Rees

Heinemann

Heinemann is an imprint of Pearson Education Limited,
a company incorporated in England and Wales, having
its registered office at Edinburgh Gate, Harlow, Essex,
CM20 2JE. Registered company number: 872828
Heinemann is a registered trademark of Pearson Education Limited

First published 2002

ISBN 978 0 435327 41 5
10 09
10 9 8 7 6 5

Designed, illustrated and typeset by Wyvern 21 Ltd, Bristol

Printed and bound in China (CTPS/05)

Index compiled by Ian D. Crane

Photographic acknowledgements
The authors and publisher would like to thank the following for permission to reproduce photographs:
David King Collection: 14 (bottom), 49, 50, 69, 71, 72, 77, 107, 111 (both), 113, 114
Roger-Viollet: 116
Topham/Novosti: 14 (top), 43
Topham/Picturepoint: 15, 20, 105
The images on pages 74, 82, 103, 143, 151, 152 and 153 are from the author's private collection.

Cover photograph: ©AKG London

Picture research by Liz Moore

Written source acknowledgements
The author and publisher gratefully acknowledge the following publications from which written
sources in the book are drawn.
F. Chuev, *Molotov Remembers* (I.R. Dee, 1993): p.110; S. Davies, *Popular Opinion in Stalin's Russia:
terror, propaganda and dissent, 1934–1941* (CUP, 1997): p.115; M. Falkus, *The Industrialisation of
Russia 1700–1914* (Macmillan Education, 1972): p.45; J. Getty, *Origins of the Great Purges* (CUP,
1985): p.114; G. Hosking, *Russia, People and Empire 1552–1917* (Fontana Press, 1998): pp.39–40;
J. Hutchinson, *Late Imperial Russia 1890–1917* (Longman, 1999): p.53; P. Kenez, *A History of the
Soviet Union from the Beginning to the End* (CUP, 1999): pp.106, 125, 146, 165; I. Kukushkin, *History
of the USSR: An Outline of Socialist Construction* (Moscow Progress, 1981): p.63; V. Kravchenko, *I
Chose Freedom: The Personal and Political Life of a Soviet Official* (London, 1947): pp.119–20; M.
McCauley, *The Khrushchev Era 1953–1964* (Longman, 1995): p.132; R. Pipes, *Russia Under the
Bolshevik Regime* (Vintage Books, 1995): pp.70, 84, 87–8; R. Sakwa, *Russia Politics and Society*
(Routledge, 1993): p.154; D. Volkogonov, *Lenin: A New Biography* (The Free Press, 1994): p.87; D.
Volkogonov: *Stalin: Triumph and Tragedy* (Harper Collins, 1998): p.96; P. Waldron, *The End of
Imperial Russia, 1855–1917* (St Martin's Press, 1997): p.52; C. Ward, *Stalin's Russia* (Edward Arnold,
1993): pp.98–9; A. Woods, *Bolshevism: The Road to Revolution* (Wellred Publications, 1999): p.52

CONTENTS

HOW TO USE THIS BOOK

This book is divided into two distinct sections. The first, and shorter section, gives an overview of the whole period of Russian and Soviet history between 1856 and 1985. It is intended as an overall introduction to the period, but is also designed to meet the requirements of AS level History. The four chapters that make up this section will provide a relatively brief narrative of events, outlining what happened during this period of Russian history. There are summary questions at the end of each chapter to enable students to reinforce their understanding of events and to provide them with a solid foundation in preparation for the more analytical work expected at A2 level.

The second section of the book is much more substantial in length and more analytical in style. This section is designed to fulfil the main aim of the book, which is to consider interpretations of the key issues of the period. While the relevant AS chapter will provide a brief background to the topic, the three parts of the A2 section will contain the analysis of key issues which will enable students to extend their understanding of the subject matter to a suitable level.

At the end of the A2 section is an assessment section, which has been designed to provide guidance for students to meet the requirements of A2 specifications when answering examination questions.

It is hoped, too, that the book will be useful to general readers who wish to find their way around what is an often complex but fascinating period of history.

AS SECTION: NARRATIVE AND EXPLANATION

CHAPTER 1

Tsarist Russia, 1856–1914

KEY QUESTIONS

- What reforms were carried out by Tsar Alexander II and how did they change Russia?
- Why was reform followed by a period of **reaction**?
- How successfully did Nicholas II rule Russia before the First World War?

CONTEXT

Following the defeat of Russia in the Crimean War of 1856, **Tsar** Alexander II (1855–81) felt compelled to introduce a series of reforms in Russia. The most important was the emancipation of the **serfs** in 1861, followed by a series of other measures designed to reform the military, legal, educational and governmental structures. However, the essentially **autocratic** nature of the Russian state remained in place and Alexander scaled down the reforms in the second part of his reign.

Following his assassination in 1881 by one of several revolutionary groups seeking a more fundamental change to Russia, Alexander's successor, Alexander III (1881–94), made it clear he was opposed to any more major reform.

Tsar Nicholas II (1894–1917) continued this approach. However, Russia was changing. Important economic developments were taking place, notably the industrialisation of parts of the country. More opposition

KEY TERMS

Reaction A political concept meaning the reversal of previously granted reforms.

Tsar A title used by male Russian monarchs since the fifteenth century. (Tsarina is the term used by female monarchs.)

Serfs The bulk of the Russian population; they were not slaves but peasants tied to the land with feudal obligations to the aristocracy.

Autocratic From 'autocracy', a system of government in which power is essentially concentrated in one person, without restrictions such as a Parliament.

groups emerged, seeking political, economic and social changes.

Defeat in war against Japan in 1904–5 sparked off the 1905 revolution. The tsar survived this scare by a mixture of repression and reforms such as the setting up of a parliamentary system, based on the *dumas*. But it seemed as if little had changed before Russia was plunged into the First World War in 1914.

REFORM AND REACTION, 1856–94

Reform
The 1860s were a crucial period for Russia. Alexander II came to the throne in 1855 as Russia was being defeated in the Crimean War. The defeat seemed to confirm that in comparison with the countries of western Europe, Russia was backward. Its society was based on serfdom, and was resistant to economic, social and political change.

The tsar was afraid that if he did not bring about change, there might be revolutionary change from below, which would destroy the centuries-old institution of tsardom, based on autocracy. Consequently, Alexander II brought in a series of reforms.

- First was the emancipation, or freeing, of the serfs in 1861. However, the serfs would have to pay the government for their land over a period of 49 years.
- The length of military service was considerably reduced.
- Censorship was relaxed.
- Local government assemblies, or **zemstvos**, were set up.
- The justice system was reformed, and made more open and independent.
- Universities were allowed to run their own affairs.

Reaction
These reforms did not satisfy many Russians. Ex-serfs found that they weren't much better off than before, while the nobility resented the loss of land and influence. Liberals wanted a greater say in government, and radicals and revolutionaries wanted a complete change in the way

radical change much more quickly than waiting for economic development to progress naturally in Russia, which was much further behind western Europe in industrialisation.

Russian society was organised. Alexander himself became much more cautious following a revolt against Russian rule by the Poles in 1863 and an attempt on his life in 1866.

The assassination of Alexander II in 1881 convinced his successor, Alexander III, that further concessions were out of the question. Influenced by his hard-line adviser **Pobedonostsev**, the new tsar reversed the 'liberal' measures of his father.

- The powers of the *zemstvos* in local government were reduced.
- Land Captains, with powers over the peasantry, were appointed.
- Censorship was extended and the government interfered more in the courts.
- Restrictions were imposed on higher education.
- *Pogroms*, or violent racial attacks, were encouraged against Jews.
- Measures were taken to suppress nationalist feeling in regions of the Russian Empire such as Poland.

These measures did not stamp out all opposition. Various groups were active against the regime at this time. They included:

- so-called '**populist**' groups, which tried to turn peasants against the regime
- anarchists, who wanted a complete overturn of society
- **Marxist** groups, taking their inspiration from the activities of Karl Marx.

In 1898, some Marxists formed the Russian Social Democratic Party. The party put its faith in the growing Russian working class to eventually replace the ruling elite with a socialist system based on workers' control of the economy.

NICHOLAS II AND THE 1905 REVOLUTION

In 1894, **Nicholas II** became tsar. Although he was weak and indecisive, he believed it was his duty to maintain the

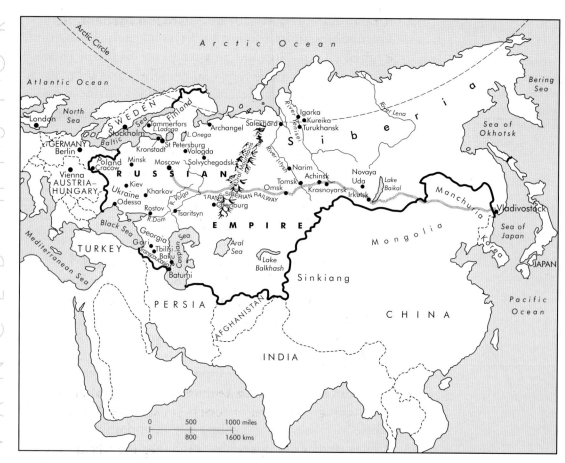

autocracy, so he dismissed calls for reform. During
his reign there were important economic and
social developments.

- Russia began to industrialise and although it remained a
  predominantly agricultural society, there were growing
  numbers of workers in the larger cities.
- There was also growing pressure on the land from an
  expanding rural population, mostly subsistence farmers.
- Of more immediate concern to the tsar was the
  Russo–Japanese War of 1904–5. The war was about
  power and influence in the Far East, but Russia's
  unexpected defeat had important consequences – a series
  of incidents known as the 1905 revolution.

Events such as **Bloody Sunday**, the *Potemkin* mutiny,
strikes and army mutinies, and the creation of a *soviet*, or
workers' council, in St Petersburg appeared to threaten the

KEY EVENT

Bloody Sunday The
massacre in January 1905 of
peaceful protesters marching
to the Winter Palace,
St Petersburg. The Winter
Palace was the main residence
of the Russian royal family,
the Romanovs.

regime. The tsar survived these uncoordinated threats mainly because:

- his October Manifesto promised reform and split the opposition
- the setting up of the *duma*, or parliament, appeared to offer hope of reform
- his new chief minister, Pyotr Stolypin, ruthlessly stamped out revolt and offered land reform to the peasantry to win their support
- there was still a lot of tacit support for the regime and the bulk of the army was still loyal.

The regime survived until 1914 and few expected revolution. Indeed, when Russia joined the First World War there was initially great enthusiasm for the struggle, as in all the countries involved.

SUMMARY QUESTIONS

1 How far did the tsarist regimes fundamentally alter Russian government or society between 1856 and 1914?

2 What forms did opposition to the regime take during this period?

3 How successful was opposition to the regime?

CHAPTER 2

War and revolution, 1914–21

KEY QUESTIONS

- What impact did the First World War have on Russia by 1917?
- What caused the February/March revolution of 1917?
- What caused the October/November revolution of 1917?
- How and why was Lenin able to consolidate Bolshevik power between 1918 and 1921?

CONTEXT

Initial Russian enthusiasm for the war in 1914 soon evaporated. The ill-prepared Russian forces suffered a series of very costly defeats against the Germans. Poor conditions and dissatisfaction with the government led to the overthrow of the tsar in February/March 1917 (February coming from the **Julian calendar**, March from the **Gregorian**). A temporary government took control.

Lenin returned to Russia from exile and turned the **Bolsheviks** into a revolutionary force, which took advantage of the increasing chaos to seize power in October/November. There was no real resistance to this revolt.

The Bolshevik struggle was only just beginning. A civil war broke out between the Bolsheviks (increasingly known as the Reds, or communists) and their opponents, the Whites. The efforts of the Red Army and measures such as War Communism (see page 9) enabled the communists to win by 1921, although Russia lay in ruins.

KEY TERMS

Julian calendar/Gregorian calendar Before 1918, Russians used the Julian calendar, which was thirteen days behind the Gregorian calendar used in western Europe. Therefore, the revolutions of 1917 were in February and October according to the Julian calendar, but in March and November respectively according to the Gregorian calendar.

Bolsheviks The name given to Lenin's Marxist party. The meaning of 'Bolsheviks' is 'those in the majority'.

KEY PERSON

Vladimir Lenin (1870–1924) Leader of the Bolsheviks from the start, Lenin spent many years before 1917 abroad or in exile. He returned to Russia after the February/March revolution of 1917 and led the Communist Party in its seizure of power in the autumn. Lenin was ruthless and unchallenged as the leader after the revolution. He basically determined Soviet policy until his death, even though he was in poor health from the early 1920s.

RUSSIA AND THE FIRST WORLD WAR, 1914–17: THE COLLAPSE OF TSARISM

Initial Russian enthusiasm for the war soon evaporated when it became clear how ill-prepared the Russians were for a long struggle against powerful opponents.

- The Russian army was large but inadequately trained.
- The army was poorly supplied and led.
- Successive defeats were marked by huge numbers of dead and captured soldiers.

Although production for the war effort was increased, the civilian sector of the economy suffered a crisis, especially of food supply to the cities. The crisis arose from:
- Inflation – prices rose faster than workers' wages and salaries.
- Communications were disrupted by administrative inefficiency and the war effort.
- Conscription of peasants created labour shortages in the countryside which badly affected landowners' estates, a prime source of food for the cities.

Attempts to improve the situation, such as setting-up War-Industry Committees of employers and workers to co-ordinate production, could not solve the problems.

- Strikes increased.
- There was growing dissatisfaction with the government's handling of the war, as ministers came and went.
- The tsar and his family were seen to be increasingly under the influence of the charismatic monk **Rasputin**.
- Even those members of society, including members of the aristocracy, who were traditional supporters of the tsar, resented the fact that they were only given a limited role in running the country and were aware that the war effort was seriously failing. They were afraid that the system on which they depended might collapse.

Although the actual events of the first 1917 revolution came as a surprise, the fact that a major outbreak of discontent occurred did not.

KEY PERSON

Grigory Efimovich Rasputin (1869–1916)
Originally a travelling pilgrim/holy man, he later developed a close relationship with the royal family.

THE REVOLUTIONS OF 1917

The February/March revolution

This revolution began as a series of disturbances in **Petrograd**. Protests against a shortage of bread coincided with strikes, with police and army units joining in the protests. With a lack of real support, the tsar was forced to abdicate. A temporary government, made up of *duma* members and calling itself the Provisional Government, took power. Unelected, it had no authority, and faced a rival in the re-formed Petrograd *Soviet*, or council, elected by workers, soldiers and sailors.

Not only did the government pass reforms and free political prisoners, but also it made the crucial decision to continue the war. The accompanying problems therefore continued.

The October/November revolution

The Bolshevik leader Lenin returned to Russia in April and persuaded his party not to co-operate with the Provisional Government but rather to work for another more radical revolution.

The government leader, Alexander Kerensky (see page 62), survived major disturbances called the July Days, but increasingly Russians were taking the law into their own hands, with soldiers deserting and peasants seizing the land. Kerensky also survived a right-wing **coup** attempt by **General Kornilov**, but lacked any effective support by the time that Lenin and **Trotsky** organised a Bolshevik coup in October/November. It culminated in an attack on the poorly defended Winter Palace.

CIVIL WAR AND THE NEW SOVIET STATE, 1918–21

The Bolsheviks had little support in Russia outside Petrograd and Moscow in 1917, but faced no organised opposition. Elections to a new parliament, the Constituent Assembly, went ahead, but when the results did not produce a Bolshevik majority, Lenin simply closed it

KEY PLACE

Petrograd The name given to St Petersburg during the years 1914–24. During 1924–91, this city was then known as Leningrad. Eventually it was renamed St Petersburg in 1991.

KEY TERM

Coup A forcible attempt to seize power.

KEY PERSON

General Lavr Kornilov Kerensky made Kornilov, who had been responsible for the tsar's arrest in 1917, commander-in-chief of the army. Kornilov decided to mobilise his troops to remove the Bolsheviks, thinking this was in the interests of the Provisional Government. However, Kerensky mistrusted Kornilov's motives and ordered his arrest for planning a military coup. Kerensky's reliance on Bolshevik support to stop Kornilov's march on Petrograd boosted the Bolshevik image and helped to fatally undermine the prestige of Kerensky's government.

Although only committed to the Bolsheviks in 1917, Trotsky, as Lenin's lieutenant, played a key role in organising the coup of October/November 1917 and the military victory over the Whites in the civil war that followed. Trotsky was widely tipped as the next leader of the USSR, but he had many enemies. Forced out of power by Stalin in the 1920s, he went into exile and was assassinated in Mexico by a Stalinist agent.

KEY EVENT

Treaty of Brest-Litovsk The treaty was signed between Lenin's government, Germany and Austria-Hungary in March 1918. It confirmed the end of Russia's involvement in the First World War, at the massive cost of Russia giving up control of its Polish, Georgian, Ukrainian and Baltic territories, and paying reparations to Germany.

down. The Bolsheviks quickly established a dictatorship and passed radical laws – for example, giving land to the peasants. They also signed the **Treaty of Brest-Litovsk**, ending the war on the Eastern front in March 1918 at the expense of giving large amounts of territory to the Germans.

Civil war and War Communism

The Bolsheviks now faced more opposition from both the left and the right, objecting to their seizure of power. The White forces – containing a mixture of military men, dispossessed landowners, national groups seeking independence from Russia and other discontented groups – fought an uncoordinated campaign under various generals.

They were supported by Allied armies of intervention. These armies were initially sent to protect supplies from falling into German hands. However, they then became committed to the anti-Bolshevik cause. Many Russians tried to keep out of the fighting altogether.

The Bolsheviks, or Reds (soon to be known as the Communist Party), ruthlessly subordinated everything to the war effort. Measures known as War Communism included nationalisation of factories and requisitioning of food from the peasants to feed Trotsky's new Red Army.

The unified Red Army command contrasted with the lack of organisation among the Whites. Both sides were ruthless, as typified by the communists' execution of the tsar and his family and White reprisals, especially against Jews and captured Red sympathisers. However, the communists made good use of their advantages. The various White armies withdrew or were defeated and the half-hearted Allies left Russia.

The communists were left in control of much of the old Russian Empire by 1921, although they faced the hostility of most major powers. Russia itself was in ruins. Agricultural and industrial production was down considerably on pre-war figures. Additionally, parts of the country were facing famine.

SUMMARY QUESTIONS

1 Why did the Russians perform relatively poorly in the
First World War?

2 What impact did this Russian performance have on
events inside Russia?

3 Why did the February/March revolution succeed?

4 Why was the Provisional Government unable to hold on
to power?

5 Why was the Bolshevik coup successful?

6 Why were the communists able to win the civil war?

CHAPTER 3

Stalin's USSR, 1921–53

KEY QUESTIONS

- How and why was Stalin able to rise to power in the 1920s?
- To what extent did the NEP help the Soviet economy recover?
- How did collectivisation and the Five Year Plans affect the Soviet economy and society?
- What were the causes and impact of the Great Terror?
- How was the USSR affected by the Second World War?
- What were the main features of Stalin's rule after 1945?

CONTEXT

After 1921, Lenin was in poor health and a fight to succeed him had already begun before his death in 1924. There was a complex struggle for influence among several contenders, notably **Stalin**, Trotsky, Grigori Zinoviev and Lev Kamenev, before Stalin emerged triumphant by 1929. Significantly, Stalin ran the Communist Party organisation, which gave him many advantages in the struggle for power.

Meanwhile, the Union of Soviet Socialist Republics (USSR) recovered from revolution and civil war, partly due to the New Economic Policy (NEP) introduced in 1921. By allowing private enterprise in agriculture and industry, a culture of profit and growth was encouraged. However, this would not bring about the cherished communist dream of an industrialised, socialist state. So there were continuing debates about the best way to achieve this. The key decisions were effectively taken in 1928.

- The process of collectivising agriculture began, with peasants being forced to join their small farms together into Party-controlled collective farms with the priority of providing food for the government's use.

- At the same time, there was a revolution in industry, with Five Year Plans being drawn up to ensure that the regime could prioritise its production needs, which meant concentrating on heavy industry.
- The entire country was mobilised to carry out this economic revolution.

During this period, the Great Terror (see page 15) took hold of the USSR, with millions of Russians disappearing in purges that resulted in imprisonment or death on a variety of charges. Former leading colleagues of Stalin were given public show trials before their disappearance. Nobody was allowed to feel safe.

The mass purges stopped shortly before the Russians were caught up in the Great Patriotic War, which started for them with the German invasion of 1941. The USSR suffered enormous human costs and material damage before the tables were turned on the Germans and the USSR was victorious in 1945.

At the end of the war, the USSR was exhausted by its efforts, but under Stalin it had also emerged, along with the United States of America, as one of the two great world powers. Stalin reimposed his iron control over all aspects of Soviet life and the USSR made a remarkable recovery by the time of his death in 1953.

THE RISE OF STALIN, 1921–9

In 1921, Lenin realised that the unpopularity of War Communism and the devastated state of Russia at the end of the civil war had to be addressed if his regime were to survive. A revolt by the sailors at Kronstadt reinforced this view. Therefore, Lenin introduced the NEP at the Tenth Party Congress. The NEP:

- stopped the requisitioning of grain
- allowed peasants to grow food for profit
- allowed limited private trade and ownership.

These measures were accompanied by a clampdown on open dissent within the Communist Party: Russia was already well on the way to becoming a one-party state. The NEP did succeed in helping to revitalise the economy, although its concessions to capitalism upset many members of the Communist Party.

Stalin's rise to power

Even before Lenin's death in 1924, there was manoeuvring for power by his leading colleagues. Trotsky seemed to be the leading contender, given his prominent role since 1917. However, Stalin was in a strong position, because as General Secretary he controlled the Communist Party machine.

KEY PEOPLE

Lev Kamenev (1883–1936) and Grigori Zinoviev (1883–1936) Kamenev and Zinoviev were leading Bolsheviks at the time of the 1917 revolution, although they initially opposed the timing of the coup. After the revolution, Kamenev ran the Moscow Party and Zinoviev ran the Comintern. Initially opposed first to Trotsky and then Stalin, both were manoeuvred out of power during the 1920s. However, Stalin had them tried and shot during the Great Terror of the 1930s.

Stalin, **Kamenev** and **Zinoviev** formed an alliance against Trotsky. Trotsky's belief in world revolution went against Stalin's policy of first building socialism in Russia. Trotsky was gradually manoeuvred out of prominence, as were his new allies Kamenev and Zinoviev. By 1927, Stalin faced opposition only from the right, led by Nikolai Bukharin, who favoured a gradual approach to industrialisation. Having defeated this opposition by 1929, Stalin was effectively dictator of the USSR and free to carry out his own policies.

ECONOMIC AND SOCIAL REVOLUTION, 1928–41

Collectivisation

Stalin launched his great economic and social revolution in 1928. A programme of collectivisation in the countryside forced peasants out of their individual farms into giant collectives, which were given the priority of delivering grain to the state.

- Millions of peasants – especially the *kulaks*, or richer ones – were deported or became industrial workers.
- Many peasants destroyed their produce rather than surrender it.
- Millions died in the famine that accompanied the chaos of collectivisation.

The ideal and the reality: the top photograph shows Ukrainian peasants learning about the advantages of collectivisation; the bottom one shows the corpses of peasants, who were victims of famine.

The Five Year Plans

At the same time, there was a massive planned programme of industrialisation.

- A series of Five Year Plans concentrated production on heavy industry necessary to build up the USSR's industrial base, and on defence.
- New industrial towns were built, but goods for ordinary people were in short supply.

The USSR rapidly became one of the world's leading industrial powers, but at great human cost, because ordinary people were made to work hard to build socialism.

The Great Terror

The assassination in 1934 of Sergei Kirov, a leading communist, was followed in 1936–8 by a series of massive purges or arrests, both of Party members and ordinary Russians.

Millions of people disappeared into labour camps or were shot, having been accused of crimes ranging from sabotage of the Five Year Plans to treason.

Former leading colleagues of Stalin such as Zinoviev, Kamenev and Bukharin were given public show trials before being executed. Stalin sowed seeds of suspicion everywhere in an attempt to keep the population vigilant but obedient. Even the army was affected, with many of its officers being purged.

The 1930s Great Terror, a satirical French cartoon showing a skeleton-like man representing the Russian people. The banner declares 'We are happy'. In the background is the NKVD (the People's Commissariat for Internal Affairs).

THE USSR AND THE GREAT PATRIOTIC WAR, 1941–5

The USSR was isolated in the 1930s. It was regarded with suspicion by non-communist states and was concentrating on its own modernisation. However, invasion of the USSR was on Adolf Hitler's agenda and the largely unprepared USSR was invaded by Germany in 1941. During the next eighteen months:

- large areas of the USSR were overrun
- millions of Red Army soldiers were killed or captured
- enormous damage was done.

The USSR survived the German attack with difficulty. Over the next three years, it gradually pushed the Germans back, ending the war in 1945 in control of much of eastern and central Europe. Stalin's prestige was increased by the war and the USSR was forced out of its isolation as an ally of the western powers. At the end of the war, the USSR, despite the devastation of the war, was one of the two great world powers, along with the USA.

THE LAST YEARS OF STALIN, 1945–53

The end of the war saw all the strict pre-war controls reimposed on the Russian people, although the scale of post-war purges was much smaller than before. Stalin was indisputably in control. He was respected as a world statesman as well as Soviet leader, although western powers were soon anxious about Soviet intentions in eastern Europe.

The remarkable feature of this period was the rapidity with which the USSR recovered economically from the war, through similar methods to those employed before 1941, particularly centralised economic planning.

SUMMARY QUESTIONS

1 How did Stalin become leader of the USSR by 1929?

2 In what ways did NEP improve the USSR's economic performance?

3 What were the effects of collectivisation?

4 How did the Five Year Plans affect the Soviet economy?

5 What impact did the Great Terror have on the USSR?

6 How was the USSR affected by its involvement in the Second World War?

CHAPTER 4

Reform and stagnation, 1953–85

KEY QUESTIONS

- In what ways did Khrushchev try to reform the USSR?
- What was meant by destalinisation and how successful was it?
- What problems did the Soviet economy and society face after Khrushchev, and how did the government deal with them?

CONTEXT

Following Stalin's death in 1953, **Khrushchev** gradually emerged as leader of the USSR. Khrushchev recognised that despite its status as a world power, reforms were necessary if the USSR were to become a more developed, prosperous society in line with communist promises. However, all his attempts to reform the Communist Party and the economy ran into opposition and problems. A policy of **destalinisation** had mixed results. In Soviet-controlled eastern Europe, destalinisation prompted serious protests against Russian influence. Khrushchev's failures, which also involved unsuccessful foreign adventures, led to his dismissal in 1964.

Khrushchev's successor was **Brezhnev**. A conservative, Brezhnev did little to reform the USSR. The economy began to stagnate, with no fundamental changes being made to the old Stalinist way of managing things. The most significant difference from Stalin's time was that ordinary people felt reasonably secure, provided they outwardly conformed to the regime's wishes.

Propaganda could not disguise the fact that the USSR faced serious difficulties, particularly in its attempts to maintain its status as a world power alongside the much richer USA.

**Mikhail Gorbachev
(b. 1931)** The first Soviet
leader whose political career
began after the Second World
War had ended. Gorbachev
achieved a remarkable
reputation throughout the
world for his negotiating skill.
He was widely regarded as the
man responsible for bringing
an end to the Cold War and
helping to achieve a relatively
smooth transition to non-
communist rule in eastern and
central Europe. However, in
the USSR itself, he was widely
regarded as weak and
indecisive, a man whose
reforms were unsuccessful and
who was mainly responsible
for the break-up of the USSR.

Following a period of manoeuvring after Brezhnev's death
in 1982, **Gorbachev**, who was committed to reform,
became leader in 1985. However, his reforms, at first
limited in scope, ended by undermining the entire
communist system.

Political reforms damaged the status of the Communist
Party. Various difficulties, notably the rise in nationalist
discontent in non-Russian regions of the USSR, eventually
resulted in the break-up of the USSR in 1991 and its
replacement by the Commonwealth of Independent States.

KHRUSHCHEV AND REFORM, 1953–64

A collective leadership took over the USSR following
Stalin's death in 1953. The leadership decided that Soviet
rule should be less rigid and based more on consent
than terror.

Khrushchev agreed that more should be done to improve
the conditions of the people. His increasing dominance
was marked by a speech to the Communist Party Congress
in 1956, in which he criticised Stalin's extreme measures.
This marked the beginnings of destalinisation, a process
that involved:

- placing restrictions on the powers of the secret police
- relaxing controls on artistic freedom and debate
- emphasising the rule of law.

While welcomed by many, this apparent relaxation
prompted expectations elsewhere. It was also partly
responsible for the Hungarian rising of 1956, brutally
suppressed by the USSR.

Khrushchev's policies were largely unsuccessful. Many
collective farms were turned into state farms in an attempt
to raise food production. This had limited impact, as did
the Virgin Lands scheme. Attempts to remove some
central controls over industry, modernise industrial
processes and provide more consumer goods all had a
limited impact, and growth rates fell.

The Virgin Lands scheme
A scheme in which large areas
of previously uncultivated
land in the USSR were turned
over to production, often with
very poor returns.

This, coupled with resentment by colleagues at Khrushchev's attempts to reform the Communist Party structure and what was seen as his humiliation in the **Cuban Missile Crisis**, led to his removal from office in 1964.

BREZHNEV AND STAGNATION, 1964–82

Brezhnev was First Secretary between 1964 and his death in 1982. During this time his power grew, as he promoted

'Grain to the Motherland', a 1978 poster typical of Brezhnev's USSR. It presents an optimistic picture of economic progress.

colleagues and was seen as a man who would not rock the boat. Under 'developed socialism', the standard of living rose and the regime seemed more relaxed for those who conformed.

However, there was a lack of any significant reform and underlying problems mounted, particularly the stagnation of the economy. This stagnation was marked by declining efficiency and failure to modernise.

THE END OF THE USSR, 1982–91

Yuri Andropov (1914–84)
Under Brezhnev, Andropov became head of the KGB and acquired a reputation for attacking corruption and bureaucracy. Following Brezhnev's death in 1982, Andropov was made General Secretary, and began some economic reforms. However, serious illness and lack of a coherent programme prevented Andropov making real progress before his death. His chief contribution was to promote new Communist Party men like Gorbachev to the leadership.

Konstantin Chernenko (1911–85) The Brezhnev old guard appointed Chernenko as General Secretary after Andropov's death mainly as a stop-gap measure to keep out Gorbachev. Widely derided as a nonentity with few ideas, the seriously ill Chernenko abandoned Andropov's campaigns against corruption and bureaucracy but was dead in little over a year after taking office, clearing the way for Gorbachev.

Following the stop-gap regimes of **Andropov** and **Chernenko** between 1982 and 1985, a reformer finally took over as Soviet leader. Mikhail Gorbachev introduced the policies of *glasnost* (openness) and *perestroika* (restructuring) in an attempt to liberalise Soviet society and encourage efficiency and economic reform. But he faced obstruction and Gorbachev himself was reluctant to concede that the Communist Party might have had its day.

His indecision added to confusion and nationalist attempts in the various republics to break away from the USSR became more serious. Although Gorbachev survived a *coup* attempt by conservatives in 1991, republics began to break away. The old Soviet Union was abolished in that year, along with the 70 year-old dominance of the Communist Party.

SUMMARY QUESTIONS

1 Why were Khrushchev's attempts at reform largely unsuccessful?

2 Why did the USSR experience growing internal problems in the post-war period and why were they not addressed?

3 Why did the USSR eventually break up in 1991?

A2 SECTION: ANALYSIS AND INTERPRETATION

PART 1

Tsarist and revolutionary Russia, 1856–1924

KEY QUESTIONS

- Why did Alexander II become a reformer?
- How significantly did the reforms of the 1860s affect Russian government, society and the economy?
- Was Alexander II a liberal?
- To what extent was the period after Alexander II one of reaction?
- How much of a threat was liberal and revolutionary opposition to the tsarist regime?
- To what extent did Russia make economic and social progress in the latter part of the nineteenth century and the first decade of the twentieth century?
- Why did the tsarist regime survive the 1905 revolution?
- How successful were the regime's measures in restoring stability after 1905?
- How stable was the tsarist regime in 1914?
- Why was Russia's performance in the First World War so disastrous and what impact did this have on Russia?
- Was the February/March revolution spontaneous or organised?
- Was the Provisional Government the architect of its own downfall?
- Why was the first revolution of 1917 followed so swiftly by a second?
- How did the Bolsheviks secure themselves in power between 1918 and 1921?
- To what extent was 1921 a significant date in the history of Soviet Russia?
- How significant was Lenin's contribution to the success of the Russian revolution?
- To what extent had the Bolsheviks transformed Russia by the time of Lenin's death in 1924?

CONTEXT

Because in historical terms the break-up of the USSR in 1991 was a relatively recent event, it is not easy to look back over the history of Russia since the mid-nineteenth century with perspective. It was even more difficult for historians writing during the period 1856–1985 itself to achieve perspective, in light of the ideological controversies which followed the 1917 revolution. Whilst claiming objectivity, western historians were themselves influenced by events which they lived through, such as the Cold War; whilst Soviet historians were obliged by their government to adopt a particular ideological stance. After 1985, the unearthing of more material from old Soviet archives further influenced interpretations. Whilst recognising that interpretations will continue to change, this section will consider some of the key issues of this period of Russian history, as they emerged or developed over a period of more than one hundred years.

Marxism and socialism

One of the key questions is how the Communist Party itself conceived the historical development of socialism. The Party line was that the ultimate victory of socialism in Russia was inevitable.

Whilst the actions of individuals like Lenin were clearly important, the Party believed that key developments depended on the working out of impersonal economic and social forces, which ultimately had a momentum of their own. This confidence was based upon communist interpretations of Marx's own reading of history. This described the transition of feudal into capitalist society.

Marx had in mind the development of a state, such as Britain, which gradually changed from a serf-based medieval society into the thrusting expansionism of a post-feudal capitalist economy. This development was based upon the accumulation of capital, the search for markets, and by the nineteenth century, the rapid expansion of industry in ever larger units as business entrepreneurs and the middle class sought to expand their profits, on the backs of a growing class of industrial workers. For Marx, such a state, whilst providing material benefits unknown in a previous era, contained the seeds of its own destruction. The growing class of workers, the proletariat, would eventually take over the state in order to enjoy the fruits of their own labour rather than allow them to line the pockets of the capitalists or owners.

Although Marx, writing in the mid-nineteenth century, did not base his analysis on the Russian economy (which he regarded as primitive in comparison with Britain, France or Germany), his ideas were seized upon by small groups of Russian intellectuals and activists such as Lenin towards the end of the century. They were living during a period when Russia was beginning to industrialise, albeit on a small scale, so there was, for the first time, evidence of a proletarian class developing in a few centres such as St Petersburg and Moscow. Marxism also had the attraction of being a visionary philosophy: it gave hope to its adherents because it promised them that the historical process of which they were a part, and of which they approved, could not be stopped.

Russian Marxists, like Lenin, accepted that to a large extent feudalism was the basis of a large section of the Russian economy until late into the nineteenth century. Even after the emancipation of 1861, the majority of ex-serfs remained tied to the land by redemption payments and poverty. Capitalism in Marxist terms was developing slowly. To make Marxism more relevant or immediate, one of Lenin's major adaptations was to develop the theory of the elite Party, which would organise the new but growing working class and lead it to a revolution. This would create a workers' state and lead to socialism, with the state taking over the means of production in the interests of the working class. Instead of waiting for socialism to arrive through natural historical development, Lenin's Party would help the process along. Even so, few Marxists (or Marxist-Leninists) expected to see a successful revolution in their lifetime.

Many western historians have argued that there was nothing inevitable about the 1917 revolution, or at least its outcome. Major developments in Russia, including industrialisation and the First World War, could have resulted in several possible scenarios. Even if some of them involved the overthrow of tsardom, this did not automatically mean the triumph of Bolshevism rather than the establishment of some sort of parliamentary regime, or more likely in the circumstances of 1917 Russia, a military dictatorship.

Similarly, although the Bolsheviks managed to establish themselves in power, this did not mean that the kind of economic and social revolution of the type introduced by Stalin, and which remained the basis of the USSR for the rest of its existence, was bound to follow. However, anti-Soviet historians tended to argue that Stalinist excesses were inherent in the nature of Bolshevism and the ruthless manner in which it came to power.

Some of the key themes which appear and reappear in the period 1856–1985 are as follows:

- autocracy and the rule of law
- ideology and conformity
- modernisation and economic development.

AUTOCRACY AND THE RULE OF LAW

Throughout the period 1856–1985, Russia was ruled by authoritarian, autocratic regimes which expected conformity with the ideology of the ruling elite. The only exception was the brief period between the fall of tsarism in February 1917 and the Bolshevik take-over in October. During this time Russia briefly flirted with the idea of a western-style parliamentary democracy, although ironically the elections necessary to create a genuinely representative system were postponed because of the war situation.

Tsarist autocracy

All Russian tsars were autocrats. Notable Russian tsars such as Peter the Great (1682–1725) and Catherine the Great (1762–96) had made some changes to a state which appeared politically, economically and socially backward compared to western European powers like Britain and France. However, the changes made by these tsars had been largely superficial, affecting court life rather than the lives of Russia's peasant population. Russia's rulers strengthened their borders, preached a kind of enlightenment and introduced a veneer of western culture. However, they also strengthened their power, and in other respects Russia remained inward looking, with its unique social structure (serf-based in large areas of the country), its own brand of Orthodox Christianity and even its own calendar.

Autocracy tolerated no compromise. Nicholas I ascended the Russian throne in 1825 after surviving the Decembrist Revolt against tsarist rule. He based his reign on three fundamental principles:
- **Orthodoxy.** This meant his divine right to rule, in alliance with the church.
- **Autocracy.** This meant rule by himself and his advisers. The tsar was to be a stern but just father figure to his subjects.
- **Nationality.** This meant the promotion and protection of Russian culture against alien influences.

In many respects these principles remained the government's defence in Russia, both before and after 1917. However, the tsar was replaced by the Communist Party and the ideological justification for the authority of the regime had a material rather than spiritual philosophy underpinning it. The soviet regime under Stalin created another principle: that of modernisation, at least in economic affairs. Ultimately the attempt by Stalin's successors to maintain autocracy and orthodoxy (communist orthodoxy rather than Romanov orthodoxy), whilst simultaneously trying to expand and modernise the Soviet economy and keeping the state free from corrupting 'liberal', 'capitalist' or other 'western' influences, created great strains which helped to tear the USSR apart by the late-twentieth century.

Communist autocracy

Tsarist Russia remained an autocratic state throughout its history. Alexander II toyed with the idea of introducing a more representative government but was killed before introducing substantial changes. Experiments such as Nicholas II's *dumas* made no significant dent in the tsar's powers. After the October Revolution the autocratic principle remained in place.

Lenin's principle of democratic centralism meant that although there was debate among leading Party members, once a decision had been made, the Party was expected to implement it. The rest of the population was also expected to conform, since the Party claimed to be guiding the interests of the 'socially useful' members of society, that is, the peasants and the workers.

Although in Soviet Russia there was a formal state structure and there were periodic elections, all key decisions were made by leading members of the Communist Party. The decisions were usually reached by consensus in the *Politburo*. However, Stalin ruled by fear as much as consensus, and was perhaps the ultimate autocrat. He largely dispensed with *Politburo* meetings and dealt with leading Party and government figures on an individual face to face basis. Whereas the authority of the tsars rested on the principle of divine right, successful General Secretaries in the USSR after Lenin – whose authority was never seriously challenged before his illness – had to secure their power by promoting their own supporters. Khrushchev paid the price for not retaining sufficient support from leading colleagues, and was dismissed. Brezhnev kept support because he looked after the interests of the Party elite.

IDEOLOGY AND CONFORMITY

For their authority, Russian tsars relied upon a combination of traditional deference, the religious mystique attached to the office, and the support of the army and other organs of state security to repress opposition to their rule. Although communist leaders did not bring the mystique of tsardom to their office, some, notably Stalin and Brezhnev, encouraged the development of personality cults around themselves. It was a Russian tradition which died hard: even in post-Soviet Russia, the Russian President Putin developed a cult of personality.

The fundamental difference between the tsarist and communist approach to conformity was the more pervasive, sophisticated and ultimately more brutal nature of the state security machine under communism. It was far more totalitarian in nature: not only was there an extensive security network to suppress any overt dissent, but extensive propaganda was used to create and sustain support for the regime which went far beyond anything in tsarist Russia.

Religion was tolerated although discouraged by the Communist Party, and its own political philosophy provided an alternative world-view. There was a strong messianic or utopian component to Marxism-Leninism, based upon a materialist philosophy: a communist, classless society was held up as a distant but ultimately achievable goal and was used to justify calls for sacrifice by the Soviet people. Heaven on earth might be achieved – but not yet. The Party never claimed that Russia had achieved communism. It was working towards socialism. Khrushchev declared that this had been achieved and that Russia was about to enter an era of communist abundance. His successor Brezhnev was more cautious, proclaiming the doctrine of Developed Socialism instead.

To proclaim the triumph of communism would have meant the withering away of the state and all its organs of power, including the Party. Communists preferred the Stalinist argument that, in a hostile world, the state must actually be strengthened rather than weakened in order to protect the fruits of socialism.

The severity and arbitrary nature of the Soviet regime was relaxed after Stalin to the extent that citizens who conformed could feel reasonably safe, and the concept of a rule of law as guaranteed in the Soviet constitution began to mean something. However, overt dissent was still not tolerated. Initiative and independent thought were not encouraged until Gorbachev introduced *glasnost* in 1985.

Nationalism and internationalism

Tsarist Russia was proud of its claims to great power status, although these proved hollow in the Russo-Japanese war and Russia suffered enormously in the First World War. The communists claimed that national rivalries were the result of international capitalist competition, and preached proletarian internationalism. National frontiers would lose their significance as the workers' revolution spread throughout the developed world.

Since this did not happen, the USSR concentrated on building up its industrial strength. Stalin in particular began to talk like an old Russian nationalist, and turned communism into a religion of national development. Inside the USSR, the concept of 'Soviet man' was promoted in an attempt to dilute differences between nationalities within the USSR. There was also a sustained campaign against foreign influences, particularly in the atmosphere of the Cold War. The attempt to reject these influences was reminiscent of the Slavophils of the nineteenth century.

MODERNISATION AND ECONOMIC DEVELOPMENT

Since Marxism-Leninism was a materialist philosophy, perhaps it is right to focus upon modernisation and economic development as the key indicator of continuity and change during this period.

In 1856 Russia was a peasant-based economy, technologically backward and characterised by low levels of productivity compared to several other European powers. Economic weaknesses were the result of several factors: amongst them an inflexible social structure, the absence of an enterprising capitalist class, lack of investment, difficulties of geography, climate and communications. By 1985 the USSR was an industrially-based economy; evidence of a major development since 1856. The change was remarkably rapid, compared for example to the transition in Britain from an agricultural to an industrial economy in the eighteenth and nineteenth centuries. The process in Russia was rapid because it was state-driven: on a small scale in late tsarist Russia, on a massive scale under Stalin. In contrast, western industrial development depended largely upon individual and corporate initiative and the availability of private capital for investment.

On one level the process of modernisation and industrialisation was successful. Industrial advances in tsarist Russia were not sufficient to enable Russia to sustain a successful war against Germany between 1914 and 1917. Arguably, however, Stalin's industrialisation of the 1930s enabled the USSR to defeat Germany in the Second World War and achieve superpower status. Against this must be balanced the great economic, social and human dislocation involved in the process, and the inefficiency of the Soviet command economy with its emphasis on quantity rather than quality. The Soviet command economy was relatively effective in establishing the basis for heavy industry, but the lack of technical sophistication and initiative was not suited to meet the needs of a more developed economy in the late twentieth century, except in a few favoured sectors such as defence.

The long-suffering Russian peasant gained little from what modernisation there was. The freed serfs in late-nineteenth century Russia found their material condition little improved. Although granted land at the time of the revolution, their lives were disrupted by war until 1921. Although relatively free of communist control in the 1920s, the peasants' lives were radically affected by the drive for collectivisation and the imposition of Party control in the countryside. Moreover, agricultural yields remained low, and none of the Soviet regime's agricultural reforms succeeded in raising productivity significantly or stimulating the peasants' enthusiasm for their lot. Modernisation largely left the Russian peasant behind, although the regime succeeded in feeding the workers in the cities. Those in Russian cities were better off than peasants, although poor by the standards of advanced western societies.

Whether modernisation could have been more effective and less traumatic in its effects on the Russian people if Russia had followed a different political path after 1917 is an impossible question to answer, although many historians and commentators have forcibly expressed their views. As in any society, 'modernisation' – with all its political, economic and social implications – came at a price. Whether the price paid by the Russians was worth the cost is a legitimate question: however, whilst as historians we can explain the processes and try to put them in perspective, it is up to individuals to judge the morality of the decisions made.

1 How significant were the reforms of Alexander II?

THE IMPETUS FOR REFORM

The two decades after the ending of the Crimean War in 1856 were a crucial time for Russia. Although it had become a major player on the European stage during and after the Napoleonic Wars, nothing fundamental had changed within Russia itself since the reign of Catherine the Great in the late eighteenth century.

Alexander II's father Nicholas I had recognised the desirability of change, particularly to the institution of serfdom, but was concerned at the possible consequences. He remembered the Decembrist conspiracy at the start of his reign. He was concerned that in Russia's autocratic, repressive society, once reforms were begun expectations would be raised that would be difficult to satisfy without undermining the very basis of the autocracy.

Additionally, 'reform' means a change to the existing way of doing things. However, there is usually a section of society that benefits from the existing state of affairs and is therefore reluctant to change. In the case of serfdom, any reform was likely to disadvantage at the very least the nobility, which benefited from the serfs' labour and was therefore likely to resist emancipation.

It was not a problem peculiar to the mid-nineteenth century. The theme of resistance to change runs throughout Russian and Soviet history. When trying to implement much-needed reform, later Soviet leaders like Khrushchev and Gorbachev faced considerable obstruction from Communist Party members and bureaucrats who feared the loss of privilege and influence if the 'system' were to be changed.

Alexander II had other factors to consider, too. Not only had Russia's defeat in the Crimean War been humiliating, but also it revealed serious deficiencies in the industrial, financial and communications structures. These deficiencies had prevented the Russian army from being adequately supplied, even though it was fighting on its own soil. If these deficiencies were to be put right, it would be necessary to make some fundamental changes to a social structure, which, based as it was on the traditional institution of serfdom, was by nature very conservative.

Interpretations of Alexander II

In addition to the impetus provided by military defeat, historians have recognised other motives for Alexander II's decision to implement reforms.

On a personal level, Alexander had received a liberal education which made him receptive to new ideas. Ideas on reform were already current in Russia. Despite the constraints on free discussion in nineteenth-century Russia, there were on the one hand Slavophils, those who looked to Russia's own resources and inner strength for salvation. On the other hand were the 'westerners', those who sought to copy reforms from western Europe and who were talking about the need to adapt serfdom.

A contemporary 'westerner', B. Chicherin, declared that:

> *Someone bound hand and foot cannot compete with someone free to use all his limbs. Serfdom is a shackle which we drag around with us, and which holds us back just when other peoples are racing ahead unimpeded. Without the abolition of serfdom none of our problems, political, administrative or social, can be solved* (quoted in G. Hosking, *Russia, People and Empire 1552–1917*).

However, the decision to reform was still not an easy one for Alexander to make. Despite his liberal sympathies, he was also prone to apathy and indecision, and this dualism in his personality stayed with him throughout his reign. It helps to account for the different interpretations sometimes made by historians. For example, Alexander appointed the reforming minister Nikolai Milyutin, who carried through emancipation. But he also appointed reactionary ministers like Count Shuvalov.

Traditionally, historians tended to divide Alexander's reign into two broad periods:

- 1855 to the early-1860s – a period of reform
- the mid-1860s to 1881, a period of reaction.

Historian Hugh Seton-Watson wrote: 'The reign of Alexander II, which began with bright promise, and changed to dreary stagnation, ended in tragedy. The tsar-liberator was a victim of the unsolved conflict between social reform and the dogma of political autocracy' (*The Decline of Imperial Russia*).

W. Mosse wrote that 'Alexander proved himself not only a disappointing "liberal", if indeed that term can be applied to him, but ... an inefficient autocrat ... He merely succeeded in proving that a pseudo-liberal autocrat is an unhappy hybrid unlikely to achieve political success' (*Alexander II and the Modernisation of Russia*).

These interpretations have elements of truth in them, but they are also over-simplifications. Alexander was clear in his own mind that there was no contradiction between his autocratic powers, which he had no intention of giving up, and his ability to grant limited reform from above.

Again, this is a recurring theme in Russian history, from the reforms of Peter the Great to the attempts of the Soviet leaders Khrushchev and Gorbachev to make the USSR more efficient and responsive to change.

In the case of the latter two leaders, they believed that they could reform even the political system while the Communist Party retained power. Alexander believed in change, but did not intend to reduce the power of the autocracy. For example, the powers given to the *zemstvos* did not extend to control over the police. Alexander wanted to make the autocracy more efficient. Reform of serfdom, along with other reforms such as the reduction in length of military service, would help to achieve that.

Just before Alexander's assassination, when he was supposedly in a phase of reaction, he was considering further changes. These involved the creation of special commissions, including elected members, to consider economic and administrative reform. His reforming minister, General M. Loris-Melikov, reported that repression had to be accompanied by measures that 'indicate the government's attentive and positive response to the needs of the people … and which could strengthen society's trust in the government and would induce social forces to support the administration more actively' (G. Hosking, *Russia, People and Empire 1552–1917*).

The truth, surely, is that Alexander was a complex character who cannot be neatly pigeonholed into one category as a 'reformer' or 'reactionary'.

The impact of emancipation

Emancipation of the serfs was carefully thought out. Consultation had begun three years before 1861, when provincial assemblies of nobles had been invited to make proposals for reform. This revealed the essential problem: opinion was divided between those liberal minded nobles favouring the granting of full personal liberty and property rights to the serfs and those more conservatively minded nobles who wanted to retain control over the peasantry.

It was these differences that prompted the government to take the initiative and insist that freed serfs must be allowed land. However, it should also have been a further indication that when the changes were eventually made, they were bound to upset some sections of society. The government itself wanted to preserve the *mir*, or village commune, since it was part of the bureaucracy and a means of managing taxes. By retaining this structure, emancipation would not make the Russian serfs equal with peasant farmers in western Europe.

Although the Emancipation Act was passed in February 1861, the actual process of emancipation took several years to complete in stages. First the serfs were freed, although some feudal obligations continued. Then agreements were made obliging the landlords to sell, and peasants to buy, a certain amount of land. Finally, the government paid landlords for the land and then arranged for the peasants to pay redemption dues back to itself for the next 49 years.

What was the significance of this reform, which earned Alexander II the title of 'Tsar Liberator'? Initially, there was confusion and resentment at the terms. Peasants were still paying for the land they farmed. But now they paid the government and had obligations to the *mir* rather than to their previous landlords or the nobility. 'Fairness' scarcely came into the equation.

- Redemption costs varied from area to area and land distribution was unequal.
- Peasants in more fertile regions received less land than in poorer areas.
- This sometimes meant that peasants had less land to work than before.
- More than 1.5 million former serfs received no land at all.
- Some peasants bought more land, but fell into debt.

By 1881, the government itself recognised that over 60 per cent of peasants had less than the minimum amount of land necessary to sustain life. At the same time, landlords resented their loss of control over the peasants. Many aristocrats themselves fell into debt. Many sold off their land and moved into various professions.

Emancipation in perspective

What was the long-term impact of these reforms? The emancipation showed that even an autocratic and conservative regime like tsarism could be persuaded to make major reforms, although the resentments aroused also highlighted the dangers. The true significance is perhaps the impulse emancipation gave to other developments. The nobility had played an important role in local government and administering justice, but now the government had broken the old relationship between serf and noble. Hence there was a need to push forward other reforms, particularly the creation of the *zemstvos* in 1864, with an important role in local government.

In economic terms, emancipation could scarcely be regarded as a great success. The initial peasant disturbances that followed emancipation died down within two years of the original disappointment, but the economic situation of the peasantry did not improve. The *mir* continued to allocate land to peasants within the village. But it had no interest in improving yields or improving efficiency generally. This was the crucial factor: Russian farming, already hampered in some areas by infertile land and a harsh climate, continued to fall behind other European powers in terms of productivity. This was particularly serious since a considerable rise in population (from 74 million to 125 million between 1858 and the end of the century) put increasing pressure on the land. Famine and peasant disturbances began to reappear before 1900, although the bulk of the peasantry remained conservative and loyal. This was witnessed by the poor response populist groups received when they tried to stir peasants into rebellion.

Emancipation should also be analysed in the broader context of Russian history. Neither tsarist nor Soviet regimes ever solved the 'problems' of the peasantry and agricultural production.

- Stolypin had only moderate success in reforming land ownership after 1905.
- Peasant reluctance or inability to provide sufficient and stable food supplies hampered Soviet governments between 1917 and 1928.
- Stalin's crude attempt to control food production and provide a workforce for industry succeeded in so far as the Communist Party did gain control of the countryside. But agricultural inefficiency remained a serious problem.
- The countryside remained the poorest sector of the Russian economy. Successive attempts at reform by Khrushchev and later Soviet leaders never solved the 'agricultural problem'.

Therefore it would be harsh to attach too much blame to the 'Tsar Liberator' for the deficiencies of emancipation.

Other reforms

The reforms that followed emancipation were important, but their significance should not be overestimated. The creation of the *zemstvos* has sometimes been hailed as an attempt to give the population a greater say – at least in local government. However, the elected local assemblies were dominated by the nobility as a result of the three-class voting system, the government retained control of the police and provincial governors could overturn *zemstvo* decisions.

The judicial reforms of 1864 promised equality before the law, independent judges and trial by jury, but the government could still hold 'special' courts and 'closed trials' in certain cases, particularly 'political' ones. Censorship was partly relaxed, but since much of the population was illiterate, this had little impact outside a small class of intellectuals.

Military reforms were important for individual conscripts, by significantly reducing the length of service from what had almost been a life sentence. But Russian military tactics, technology and leadership were slow to modernise.

Some of these reforms – for example, granting universities the right to run their own affairs and the judicial reforms outlined on the previous page – were later reversed. Therefore although Alexander II was a reformer, itself significant in a Russian context, the practical effects of the reforms were limited.

CONCLUSION

How significant were Alexander II's reforms? They appeared to be in line with developments that had occurred in previous generations in more liberal western European states. However, the tsarist regime remained autocratic, with few restraints on its freedom of action.

The reforms raised expectations without satisfying them and in this respect were partly responsible for the growth of opposition groups, a feature in Russia throughout the next 50 years. The principle of elected representatives had been accepted in local government and even discussed as a possible development in central government. But the tsar dismissed these proposals, as well as dismissing most of his reforming ministers.

Geoffrey Hosking concluded that: 'The reforms of Alexander II went a long way towards erecting the framework for a civil society' (*Russia, People and Empire 1552–1917*). However, the government, realising the danger in what it was doing, then held back.

Russell Sherman went further in concluding that: 'Russia was transformed from a semi-feudal society into (at the least) a putative modern state' (*Russia, 1815–81*). This last judgement is probably an exaggeration, since the fundamentals of the tsarist autocracy and conservative social structure remained, as they did until the shock of revolution in 1917.

2 To what extent were movements for reform and revolution a threat to the tsarist regime before 1905?

THE CONTEXT OF OPPOSITION

As already indicated, Alexander II's reforms did not prevent opposition movements from arising, but rather encouraged them to some extent by raising expectations that were disappointed. Various opposition movements developed during the late nineteenth century, but how significant a threat to the autocracy were they?

Opposition was not a new phenomenon in Russia. In old pre-nineteenth century Russia, there had been serious differences between the tsars and the nobility. There had also been periodic revolts by the serfs. Strong tsars like Peter the Great earned fear and respect for the ruthless way in which they crushed opposition. Catherine the Great had released the nobility from the duty of compulsory service to the state and relied increasingly on a new bureaucratic class to administer the tsar's power. In the long run, this was to create further problems for the tsars as the nobility increasingly resented their loss of power and privilege, feelings that came to a head during the reign of Nicholas II. Alexander I and Nicholas I tried to tread cautiously to avoid antagonising the nobility, an important force in local government before 1861.

Opposition had emerged from other quarters. The Decembrist conspiracy of 1825 had been led by a group of army officers. They were republican. However – and this was typically Russian – they were also in favour of firm government. The revolt was crushed, but it demonstrated to the tsar that he could not take support for granted, although there was a tradition of loyalty towards the 'Little father', particularly from the peasantry.

There were Russians who disliked aspects of the regime but who never actually resisted it. Relatively few took up active opposition. To do so was a major step in a society without the means of open expression such as a free press or Parliament. People who became opponents were usually against the whole fabric of society. They were forced to become revolutionaries to express their beliefs and they had to be willing to risk imprisonment or worse. These people were relatively few in number. The authorities took them seriously and employed means such as censorship, a secret police force and informers to infiltrate, check out opposition groups and sometimes break them up.

Nevertheless, the government response should not be exaggerated. The regime at the end of the nineteenth century employed fewer secret police than the personnel of a typical modern British county police force. The forces of law and order employed by the tsars were a far cry from the apparatus of the police state developed by the post-1917 Communist Party with its extensive network of secret police, informers, propaganda and *gulag* of prison and labour camps designed to intimidate an entire population. Except in moments of major crisis such as the 1905 revolution, the tsarist regime could count on great reserves of loyalty, or at worst apathy, from the mass of the population.

TYPES OF OPPOSITION

Intellectual opposition

Intellectuals formed a very diverse group. During the 1840s, when government repression was strong, several notable Russian intellectuals were already active or beginning their careers. They included the poets Alexander Pushkin and Mikhail Lermontov, and the novelists Ivan Turgenev, Fyodor Dostoevsky and Lev Tolstoy.

These writers were very conscious of the authoritarian rule under which they lived. In their works they discussed issues of morality and personal conscience which arose in such a society. They were also patriotic in the sense of believing that Russia could have a better future. Despite government censorship, these intellectuals had considerably more artistic freedom than would be permitted later under Soviet rule. Some of them were **Slavophils**, who were defending what they believed were Russian values against imported ideas of liberalism and democracy from western Europe and the USA, and putting their faith in the peasantry as Russia's future.

Opposed to them were the so-called liberal westernisers, who despised Slavophils for their obsession with tradition and what they regarded as superstition. One of the best known westernisers was Alexander Herzen, who was steeped in western philosophy. He left Russia for good in 1847.

In the freer climate of Alexander II's early years, intellectuals increasingly represented different strands of political thought.

- Many were Slavophil, and therefore essentially conservative and nationalist.
- Some writers like Chicherin were liberal, attacking aristocratic privilege and advocating individual rights and the rule of law.
- Others like Chernyshevsky were radical, advocating a form of 'peasant socialism' based on communal landholding.
- Other Russians had liberal ideas in that they supported the notion of

KEY TERM

Slavophil The literal translation of this is 'lover of the Slavs'. The Slavs – who include Belorussians, Bulgarians, Croats, Czechs, Russians, Ukrainians, Poles, Slovaks, Slovenes and Serbs – are from various central and eastern European countries and share similar languages.

constitutional government and the rule of law, without necessarily being classified as intellectuals or opponents of the regime. They included members of the growing middle class and became more significant in the 1900s (see pages 52–3).

It is important not to overestimate the influence of intellectual critics of the regime. They were part of a small intellectual elite, not widely read or heard outside their own and student circles. However, in the disappointment that followed the emancipation of 1861 and other reforms, some of the intellectual criticism did become more strident and influenced members of the more overtly revolutionary movements of the 1870s and 1880s.

Populist opposition

What distinguished populism from the intellectual movements discussed on the previous page is that, while taking some of their initial ideas from writers, the populists were prepared to go much further in terms of actions. They believed that the end justified the means.

One of the earliest groups was Land and Liberty, formed in the early 1860s. Groups of young socialists, inspired by events such as the Paris Commune of 1871, believed that they could awaken 'the people' to the desirability of a socialist future. Groups embarked on a campaign of 'To the people', which meant travelling into villages to stir up the peasants against taxation, the shortage of land and other grievances. Their idealism had little effect. The populists were met largely with apathy or hostility by uncomprehending peasants who had nothing in common with intellectuals or students from the towns. Moreover, these groups had no organisation or co-ordination and could scarcely be considered a serious threat to the regime.

Anarchism

Anarchism, a doctrine that rejected the whole apparatus of organised government, was associated chiefly with Mikhail Bakunin. He, like the Populists, believed that the ordinary people could create a new civilisation, untainted by western ideas. An intellectual movement without wide popular appeal, anarchism did not pose a significant threat to the regime.

Terrorism

In the later 1870s, the failure of populism was evident to many radicals and a shift in activity took place. In 1876, Land and Liberty developed a proper, secret organisation. It became involved in various forms of agitation such as printing appeals and leaflets, and devoted as much time to the urban working class as to the peasantry. It also became engaged in 'disorganisational activity' – in other words, terrorism. Several prominent police and local government officials were assassinated. A more extreme breakaway group calling itself People's Will, and advocating political freedom based on a constitution, finally succeeded in assassinating Alexander II in 1881.

Inevitably, terrorist activity resulted in stimulating more publicity than intellectual activity achieved. Terrorist activities were more of a threat simply because the terrorists succeeded in killing some prominent people, including the tsar. These activities also had a symbolic value in creating martyrs for the revolutionary cause. But in practical terms there was little benefit to the revolutionary cause. There was no mass uprising by the people in response to these actions. The regime was not going to be deflected from its policies. Indeed, it responded with greater vigilance and more activity against all dissident groups. Alexander III set his face firmly against reform.

Many intellectuals despaired of change in the 1880s. Most famously, Tolstoy rejected his previous life and turned to spiritual reflection and moralising.

Marxism

The link between populism and Marxism was a group of former Land and Liberty members including George Plekhanov and Paul Axelrod, who became converted to Marxism in the 1880s. They accepted Marx's analysis that socialism was essentially an urban phenomenon that would grow as capitalism developed, and with it would grow an industrial working class, or proletariat, containing the seeds of revolution.

These Russian Marxists were shifting the radical emphasis away from the peasantry and towards the developing industrial cities of Russia. There were major philosophical arguments to be resolved. Since capitalism was at a relatively early stage of development in Russia, should Marxists be supporting this development and ignoring the workers' suffering around them, since the quicker the development took place, so the prospects for socialism grew brighter? Could the process be speeded up? Should Marxists support attempts by fledgling workers' movements like trades unions to better their conditions? Or were these simply distractions from the real task of working for revolution?

The chief attraction of Marxism for its adherents was that it appeared to be based on a 'scientific' analysis of society combined with an almost religious faith in eventual success. It appeared a movement for the future, unlike populism. In the words of Geoffrey Hosking:

> *Populism stressed the uniqueness of Russian experience and the ancient*
> *democratic institutions of the peasantry, while Marxism stressed*

universality and modernity, wishing to see Russia rejoin the European mainstream. In a sense, then, populism was Russian ethnic socialism, while Marxism was Russian imperial or Europeanised socialism. By trying to synthesise the two visions in 1917, Bolshevism created an unstable amalgam of Russian nationalism and internationalism, coloured with the messianic expectations of the revolution which would put an end to exploitation (Hosking, *Russia, People and Empire 1552–1917*).

Lenin and Bolshevism

It was Lenin who appeared to give Marxism its clearest direction, or at least in his own interpretation of Marxism. Lenin, who became the leader of the Bolshevik faction in 1903, was a master of tactics as much as philosophy. While arguing with colleagues about the philosophy of Marxism, he devoted as much attention to organisation, believing that under the repressive conditions in Russia, it was important to have a secret, disciplined, committed party. This would act as a vanguard of the working class and develop its class consciousness for when the time was ripe for revolution.

Like other revolutionary movements, the Marxists appeared to offer little threat at the time. The Bolsheviks and their rivals the Mensheviks, who supported the concept of a more broadly based party, were small groups with little influence. Many of their leaders were arrested and imprisoned or exiled. Other groups like the Socialist Revolutionaries, which were peasant based, were larger but equally ineffectual.

CONCLUSION

How much of a threat to the regime were these intellectual and political developments? Certainly there was a growing change of emphasis as the nineteenth century progressed. Many more people than before questioned the principle of autocracy as the basis for government in Russia, particularly as the system seemed reluctant to reform itself from within. Partly these perceptions came from acquaintance with western ideas of liberalism and constitutional government. But there were other critics of the regime who rejected these trends completely.

Divisions were rife within the revolutionary camp. The regime had relatively little difficulty in dealing with overt expressions of opposition, despite isolated instances such as the assassination of Alexander II. Of greater long-term threat was the fact that, gradually, whole social groups previously loyal to the autocracy became, to a greater or lesser degree, alienated.

These groups included many nobles and peasants. While not prepared to take up arms against the regime, they were increasingly less willing to give it their full support in the absence of more concessions for themselves. In 'normal' times this seemed less significant. But in critical moments this decline in support might prove more serious. It almost proved fatal in 1905. In fact, it *did* prove fatal in 1917 when the regime faced a major crisis and could no longer call on support it had once taken for granted.

3 How significant was economic and social change in Russia before 1914?

BACKGROUND

Until and beyond 1914, Russia had primarily an agriculturally based economy and society. Up to four-fifths of the population made its living directly or indirectly from agriculture. The abolition of serfdom in 1861 in theory made industrial development more feasible, since the population was less tied to the land. Also there were many ex-serfs without any land who were looking for work. A potential industrial workforce was available. One economic historian therefore asserted that 'the year 1861 can in many respects be taken as marking the beginning of Russia's modernisation' (Falkus, *The Industrialisation of Russia 1700–1914*).

Certain industries were relatively developed in Alexander II's reign – notably textiles and sugar. There was also considerable railway expansion, at a rate of 400 per cent between 1868 and 1878, although this was mainly the result of private enterprise rather than state intervention, which became significant later. The heavy industry and consumer goods industries began to expand at about 5 per cent a year from the 1860s, assisted by a considerable rise in the number of banks and other financial institutions.

However, the limitations of these developments should be emphasised. Expansion was from a small industrial base and was punctuated by periods of depression. The economy was still dependent on agriculture: not only did the bulk of the population live from the land, but also the system of land ownership discouraged agricultural innovation. The *mir* dictated the method of cultivation and in effect owned the land, parcelling it out in small quantities and frequently redistributing it. Peasants had little incentive to farm efficiently, although they had to try to make a living for themselves.

A CHANGING ECONOMY AND SOCIETY?

In recent years, there has been a controversy among historians about the extent to which emancipation made the economy more fluid and responsive to change.

On the one hand, the situation remained inflexible. If peasants got permission from the *mir* to leave the village, they were required to pay taxes while away and could be recalled by the *mir*. Some historians have argued that this discouraged movement. Others have argued that there is more and more evidence in the late nineteenth century of peasants travelling in order to find work in factories and on the railways, while increasing numbers bought and sold land. Therefore, society may have been becoming more fluid. Clearly the evidence is somewhat contradictory. It is likely that some peasants developed wider horizons from their experience of primary education, military service outside their region and prospects of more varied work.

On the other hand, many peasants remained conservative in outlook, retaining an inflexible faith in the Orthodox Church and being very tied to their immediate community. One generalisation that can be made is that even for peasants whose horizons were widening, there were no opportunities to express themselves politically. Therefore there was little sense of belonging to a wider political community beyond the village and no sense of membership of what Hosking called the 'civic nation'.

Early industrialisation – workers in a boiler factory, c.1890.

A peculiar feature of social development in Russia was the way in which many peasants became what have been described as 'economic amphibians' or 'peasant proletarians', finding work in urban factories for part of the year and returning to the village at key times such as harvest. In 1910, almost 70 per cent of the inhabitants of Moscow and

St Petersburg could still be classified as 'peasants'. This search for seasonal work was not surprising, since the rising rural population, especially in the fertile regions of central and western Russia, put pressure on already scarce food supplies.

Despite the transitory nature of the urban workforce, it is still possible to talk of a developing 'working class' in the two generations before 1914. In a few centres of industry the working class population expanded considerably. Concentrations of workers in poor housing and factories provided recruiting material for groups like the Bolsheviks, particularly since workers' conditions scarcely improved in this period. The right to strike was established in 1905 and the right to form trades unions in 1906. But there were limits to their effectiveness.

AN INDUSTRIAL REVOLUTION?

Industrial development would be crucial in helping Russia to develop a strong economic base. Industrial power was the basis for military power and a thriving economy, as already proved by Great Powers like Britain and the new Germany. Even the conservative Russian government realised this, and a particular feature of Russian economic development was the degree of government intervention. This was far more extensive than in other Great Power economies, but very much in keeping with Russian tradition. It ran right through from Peter the Great to communist attempts to manage every aspect of industrial life through a 'command economy' expressed in Five Year Plans.

There were several aspects of industrialisation:

- financial – industrial expansion had to be financed; this was achieved through setting up a state bank in 1860 to provide credit, through the development of numerous private banks and through attracting foreign investment, especially to build railways
- reforming taxation
- tariff protection for Russian industry
- railway construction, including the **Trans-Siberian Railway**.

These developments are primarily associated with Ministers of Finance Ivan Vyshnegradsky (1887–92) and Sergei Witte (1892–1903). Witte in particular took a long-term strategic approach to the economy, arguing that the state must play a major role in promoting industrial development in order to compete with other world powers. In a famous memorandum of 1899, he wrote: 'Russia is an independent and strong power. [It] has the right and the strength not to want to be the eternal handmaiden of states which are more developed economically.'

THE SIGNIFICANCE OF RUSSIA'S ECONOMIC DEVELOPMENT IN THE TWENTY YEARS BEFORE THE FIRST WORLD WAR

In dealing with the debate about the significance of Russia's economic development prior to the First World War, there are arguments that focus on the success of the industrialisation strategy and those that focus on the limitations of economic growth.

Arguments that focus on the success of the industrialisation strategy

Some of the figures are impressive. Industrial growth expanded at over 8 per cent a year in the 1890s. During the 1890s, the rail network almost doubled in size, making it second only to the USA. After 1900, the continuing industrial expansion began to be as much self-generated as state-sponsored. Between 1906 and 1913, the growth rate in industry picked up again, at more than 6 per cent per annum. One historian argued that:

> In three decades [by 1913] *Russia had industrialised on a more rapid scale than any other country during that period. [Its] industrialisation, from being 'forced' in the 1890s in a manner reminiscent of Peter the Great, was becoming more spontaneous by the outbreak of the war ... No explanation of Russia's industrial growth under the Soviet regime after 1917 would be complete without taking into account the industrial base inherited from tsarist days* (Falkus, *The Industrialisation of Russia 1700–1914*).

Arguments that focus on the limitations of economic growth

The rate of growth was not uniform. For example, the rate of growth fell off considerably between the late 1890s and 1905, years marked by bankruptcies and falling output. During this period other economies expanded at a faster rate and Russia actually slipped down the international table of industrial ranking. In 1913, industry still contributed only 20 per cent of national income and only 18 per cent of Russians lived in towns. Russia was Europe's largest debtor nation by 1914 and much of the debt was never paid off.

CONCLUSION

In purely economic terms, despite Falkus's argument above, the effects of industrialisation were limited. Russia was not able to compete as an industrial force with other powers until Stalin's massive and forced industrialisation drive of the late 1920s and early 1930s. The early rapid gains in production were due mainly to the fact that Russia was starting from a very limited base. On the other hand, there *was* a base, however backward, in relation to other Great Powers, which enabled Russia to fight in the First World War for three years as a major force.

Less easy to evaluate is the social impact of industrialisation. The sale of consumer products increased considerably in the years before the war. Yet there is also considerable evidence of workers continuing to live and work in primitive conditions. The number of strikes grew between 1912 and 1914, and there were relatively few attempts to improve urban conditions. Just as members of the nobility, middle class and peasantry all had grievances against the regime either for material reasons or because they lacked political influence, so few workers benefited directly from the industrial expansion that did take place – as was to be the case in the Soviet period also.

4 How stable was the tsarist regime in 1914?

ISSUES OF INTERPRETATION

There has been considerable debate about how stable the tsarist regime actually was on the eve of war in 1914, given the fact that it collapsed three years later. This raises some major issues of interpretation.

- To what extent had the regime recovered from the shock of the 1905 revolution by 1914?
- Was the apparent recovery such that the regime might have expected to enjoy long-term survival?
- Were the concessions made by the regime after 1905 such that this recovery had real substance?
- Was Russia developing economically and socially in a way that would promote stability?
- Could the regime itself adapt to these changing conditions?
- Would the regime have survived but for the disasters of the First World War?

This war was so profound in its impact that all major combatant nations were seriously affected, including victorious ones, so it was scarcely surprising that the tsarist regime ran into serious difficulties. The two most extreme interpretations, at opposite ends of the spectrum, are these.

- The post-1917 Soviet version of history is that the regime lacked any basis for long-term survival even in 1914. In terms of a Marxist analysis, Russia was gradually changing from a feudal to a capitalist society. There were debates about the speed of the process. However, there was basic agreement that, because of the fundamental inner contradictions of capitalism, a socialist society would eventually emerge. While the First World War created additional economic and social pressures, these alone could not account for the collapse of tsarism. This would have happened eventually in any case; the war simply speeded up the process. The Bolsheviks were making good progress in building up support among the working class even before the war.
- The 'anti-Soviet' version of history is that the tsarist regime had a lot of factors in its favour in 1914. But for the disastrous involvement in war, there is every reason to suppose that tsarism could have survived, particularly if it adapted to changing circumstances. Russia was making considerable economic and social progress by 1914. It was the war that rudely shattered this progress and the long-term prospects for success

rather than any 'internal contradictions' of the economy or society under tsarism.

Interpretations somewhere between these two extremes usually run on the lines of the following.

There were some significant developments in Russia in the years before 1914, although it is difficult to assess exactly how 'stable' the regime was in 1914. It was essentially the disastrous war experience that brought down the regime in 1917. But this need not automatically have led to the long-term outcome of a communist take-over and the creation of the world's first socialist state. Before 1914 there was evidence of a limited willingness to adapt by the regime.

The difficulty of assessing all interpretations of 1914 is that we are in the realms of hypothesis. Historians cannot know what might have happened had the war not broken out or had Russia's performance been significantly better. They can only consider the evidence available and make informed, but nevertheless speculative, judgements.

THE SIGNIFICANCE OF THE 1905 REVOLUTION

The events of 1905 are briefly outlined on pages 4–5. It's worth emphasising, however, that 1905 was not a revolution in the conventional sense of being a prepared coup against the state by a particular group with specific aims. The best-known events of the revolution were not co-ordinated. While they were (to some extent) sparked off by each other and the catalyst of Russia's defeat in the war against Japan, they had different origins.

The marchers trying to petition the tsar outside the Winter Palace on Bloody Sunday were not seeking to overthrow him. They were seeking redress for certain grievances and reserved their hostility for tsarist officials. The petitioners expressed their loyalty to the tsar and were not revolutionaries trying to overthrow the regime. Some of the mutineers on the *Potemkin* may have had political aims, but the mutiny was as much a protest at poor service conditions as an awakening of political consciousness.

Revolts among subject peoples of the empire were evidence of awakening national feeling against **russification**. But they had no connection with the activities of the unrepresentative political activists in the Petrograd *Soviet*. The 1905 revolution was a series of disparate revolts and protests, which of course largely accounts for its failure, although this was also due to the regime making intelligent concessions. The granting of the

KEY TERM

Russification An attempt to 'Russianise' – particularly in terms of language and religion – non-Russians living in the Russian Empire.

The arch priest of reaction: Konstantin Pobedonostev, adviser to Alexander III and Nicholas II (from a revolutionary journal published in 1905). The caption reads 'The evil genius of Russia'.

„СТРѢЛЫ"

Журналъ сарҡастическій, безстрашный и безпощадный.

Сотрудникамъ приказано:

Цѣна 5 коп   Патроновъ не жалѣть и холо-
стыхъ залповъ не давать.

Злой геній Россіи.

October Manifesto with its promise of reforms immediately reinforced the existing split between moderate liberals seeking constitutional reform and the minority of die-hard revolutionaries intent on creating a new political, social and economic order.

Lenin justified the revolution as a 'dress rehearsal' and the writer Maxim Gorky declared that 'this is the beginning of the end of the bloodthirsty tsar'. But in 1914, Lenin was marginalised and extremely pessimistic about the prospects for revolution. Meanwhile, the tsar regained most of his standing and could count on traditional reserves of loyalty from much of the population.

Въ мірѣ есть царь. Онъ безпощаденъ. ГОЛОДЪ — названье ему.

Издатель С. М. Прохоровъ.

A drawing from a revolutionary journal of 1905. The caption reads 'In this world there is a tsar. He is without pity. HUNGER is his name'.

REFORM AND REPRESSION AFTER 1905

Analyses of events after 1905 usually focus on the activities of the new *dumas*, and the mixture of repression and reform associated with Stolypin, the driving force in the administration between 1906 and his assassination in 1911.

The *dumas*

The *duma* was not a law-making parliament in the western sense and ministers were not accountable to it. The tsar could dismiss it at will and manipulate the elections to influence its composition, which he did for the third *duma*. Therefore the *dumas* were only a weak constitutional check on the tsar. They did not satisfy the political ambitions of liberals who wanted a greater share in the political process. In any case, members of the *duma* were divided in their views. On the right were the United Nobility, concerned to protect the status of the aristocracy. The Octobrists wanted a constitutional monarchy, but had a rudimentary organisation. The more organised Kadets were not satisfied with the concessions made, while the Social Democrats could never be satisfied and were mostly excluded from the *duma* or boycotted it. Workers and peasants generally did not feel any involvement in the *duma* and other representatives from national groups and the peasantry were not organised and had little voice.

The *dumas* could provide some embarrassment for the regime, but little else. There is no evidence that the tsar was considering further serious constitutional reform in 1914, and therefore no reason to suppose that Russia was in any foreseeable future likely to move peacefully to a system of genuine constitutional monarchy.

Stolypin

Stolypin's repressive measures against those involved in the 1905 revolution are generally held to have been effective in helping to restore order, especially in the countryside. More controversial are his agrarian reforms, designed to build up a class of prosperous, independent peasants who would provide a bulwark of loyal support for the regime. Removing the authority of the *mir* and the land captains and encouraging peasants to consolidate and develop their holdings was an imaginative policy from someone not noted for his reforming zeal.

However, the actual effects were limited. After some initial enthusiasm, applications from peasants for permission to break away from the commune fell off after 1909, except in the more fertile areas of South Russia and Ukraine where the prospects for entrepreneurial farming seemed better. Crop yields remained poor and a rising population continued to put pressure on the land. About one-quarter of the peasants owned their own land by 1916, but it is very doubtful whether the reform would have gone a significant way towards solving the agricultural 'problem', particularly since the measures soon lost their impetus anyway.

KEY EVENT

Lena Goldfields Massacre In 1912, workers at the goldfields, situated on the river Lena (in Eastern Siberia), were massacred after petitioning for improved employment conditions.

While many peasants may have retained some loyalty to the regime, little was done to strengthen the loyalty of other classes, particularly in the towns. The powers recently given to trades unions were suppressed, and employers clawed back improvements in wages and working conditions forced from them in 1905.

These indications, along with the infamous **Lena Goldfields Massacre** in 1912 and the growing number of industrial strikes deemed 'political' in the months before the war, do not suggest a recipe for long-term stability.

Intelligent Russians were aware of the dangers. Member of the State Council Peter Durnovo wrote a memorandum to the tsar in February 1914 outlining his fears for Russia in the event of war. He warned: 'We must note the insufficiency of our military supplies, and our excessive dependence upon foreign industry.' If Russia chose the wrong side (he meant England), there would be 'a weakening of the monarchical principle', and, in the event of defeat …

> … a social revolution which … will inevitably degenerate into a socialist movement. Russia will be flung into anarchy such as it suffered in 1905–6. It will start with all disasters being attributed to the government, resulting in revolutionary agitation. The defeated army will prove to be too demoralised to serve as a bulwark of law and order. The legislative institutions, lacking real authority, will be powerless to stem the rising popular tide, which they themselves had aroused, and Russia will be flung into hopeless anarchy, the outcome of which cannot even be foreseen.

Rasputin also advised against the dangers of war.

CRISIS OR NO CRISIS?

Historians have long argued whether or not the tsarist regime was increasingly unstable in 1914, as the extracts below show.

Arguments supporting the view that the regime was increasingly unstable

> Russian society was fragmenting in the 60 years after 1855: the traditional rural relationship between lord and master was broken by emancipation and, as the nobility ran down their landholdings, any moral authority which they may have held decreased. Urban workers and the new urban middle classes existed only fitfully as coherent groups, and although bonds were growing inside urban society, by 1914 neither worker nor businessman could claim to be part of a unified group (Waldron, The End of Imperial Russia, 1855–1917).

> Objectively the situation was ripe for revolution … The [Bolshevik] party was now stronger than ever … On the eve of the Fist World War, the revolutionary movement was even stronger and more widespread than in 1905. More important still, the consciousness of the working class was on a qualitatively higher level … It can be calculated with a large degree of certainty that the Bolsheviks had the support of at least three-quarters of the organised working class (Woods, Bolshevism: The Road To Revolution).

Woods bases these calculations on the success of Bolsheviks in winning places in *duma* elections and in organised workers' groups.

Arguments against the view that the tsarist regime was unstable in 1914

The revival of militancy, while undeniably important, was scarcely the beginning of an organised revolutionary effort ... Western historians have disproved earlier Soviet claims that the militancy was planned or directed by the Bolsheviks; nor, for that matter, was it the work of other socialist parties. The typical pre-war militant in the Imperial capital was likely to be a skilled metalworker who distrusted intelligentsia organisers as much as he despised policemen and factory inspectors (Hutchinson, *Late Imperial Russia 1890–1917*).

CONCLUSION

According to Orlando Figes, any idea that the regime might have been able to reform itself before 1914 but for the assassination of Stolypin is misguided: 'This optimistic view rests on the assumptions that Stolypin's reforms were succeeding in their aims; and that they were capable of stabilising Russia's social system after the crisis of 1905. Both assumptions are patently false' (Figes, *A People's Tragedy: The Russian Revolution 1891–1924*).

Can we be certain how stable the regime was in 1914? And did it have the inner strength to avert revolutionary change? Since the First World War proved so catastrophic for Russia, we cannot be certain, since the regime ran out of time. On page 45 we saw evidence of the limitations of Russia's industrial development. In 1914, Russia was behind Germany, Britain and the USA in the production of coal, iron and steel, and in the value of foreign trade.

Added to economic factors are less quantifiable ones such as the weakness of Nicholas II's personality. His hesitancy and obstinacy made him incapable of distinguishing between good and poor advice. In particular, the tsar's determination to uphold the principle of autocracy and privileges of the landed nobility overrode the views of those bureaucrats who did recognise the need for reform.

On the other hand, organised opposition was still in its infancy. Industrial unrest was mostly confined to St Petersburg, and the public mood was less volatile than it had been in 1905, a crisis the tsar had survived. Nicholas II was confident of the military's support. Although many Russians were dissatisfied, and there were evident stresses and strains in society, there was as yet no catalyst to force the issue, as there was to be once Russian involvement in the First World War created new problems and exacerbated existing ones.

5 Why was Russia's performance in the First World War so disastrous?

THE CONTEXT OF THE WAR

The outbreak of war in 1914 brought a genuine but fragile unity to Russia. The tradition of loyalty to the state in a time of crisis was strong, and there was optimism that Russia would win. Strikes and demonstrations ceased, along with criticisms of the government. Had the regime been able to sustain some early successes before the formidable German war machine began to take its toll, this early enthusiasm might have been sustained.

Was the optimism justified? Although industrial and agricultural productivity had not increased as quickly in Russia as in some countries, the advances were not negligible. Criticism of Russia's war performance should be tempered by the fact that Russia was able to hold a front line against powerful armies for three years of war. This was a considerable achievement considering the broader context of Russia's position. Since Russia entered the war with a level of gross national product per person below that of its rivals, including Austria-Hungary, the effort to sustain the war put enormous pressure both on the economy and on the military and the administrative structures.

In a broader context, Russia's international position had declined despite its success in expanding its frontiers eastwards across Asia in the nineteenth century.

- Defeats in wars in the Crimea (1854–6) and against Japan (1904–5) cast doubts on Russia's military capability in a major struggle.
- The Polish revolt of 1863 and the emergence of Germany on the international scene raised concerns about the security of Russia's western frontiers.
- Awareness of Russia's weakness in the aftermath of the defeat against Japan and the 1905 revolution encouraged the German–Austrian alliance to pursue its ambitions in the Balkans more aggressively. This in turn forced the Russian government to stand up to militarily superior opponents.
- Nicholas II did not want war in 1914. Russia's military leaders knew that the German army was stronger than their own. They also knew that to delay a conflict would be better for Russia, because its great plan to improve the army was not due to be completed until 1917/18. However, political considerations overrode military caution. Russia's

rulers felt that the very legitimacy of the regime was at stake in 1914, and that the humiliation of backing down in the international crisis of 1914 would fatally damage Russia's international standing both with Great Power allies and with client states like Serbia, and would encourage rivals.

HOW DISASTROUS WAS RUSSIA'S PERFORMANCE?

Once the war had begun, Russia's problems increased on both the military and the home fronts. Historians usually focus on the significant weaknesses of the Russian war effort.

KEY CAMPAIGNS

Brusilov offensive The Russian offensive of 1916, named after General Brusilov, initially achieved great success against the Austrians and helped encourage Romania to join the war on the Allied side. However, the offensive was eventually stopped when German forces bolstered the Austrian army. The Brusilov offensive cost the Russians a million casualties for no perceptible gains.

The Somme and Verdun Major battles in the trenches on the Western Front in 1916, involving the German, French and British armies.

On the military front, the Russians had huge manpower. But the soldiers were sometimes ineffectually led and, most importantly (especially in the early phases of the war), were inadequately supplied. Uniforms and rifles were often in short supply, and the artillery did not have sufficient shells. Supplies improved considerably by 1916. By then, though, the rot of defeat and growing demoralisation had already set in. The Russian armies were also hampered by lack of a coherent command structure.

However, some more recent interpretations have attempted to balance the depressing analysis outlined above. Not just the Russian army, but frequently other armies (including the British and French), proved inferior to the German army, and Russian armies frequently did well against the Austrians and even against the Germans in particular campaigns such as the initial stages of the **Brusilov offensive** in 1916. As late as 1917, there were still grounds for optimism that the Allies could win the war. The massive campaigns of 1916 – **the Somme**, **Verdun** and the Brusilov offensive – had seriously weakened the Central Powers, and the USA was close to entering the war.

Unfortunately for the Russian regime, given the nature of much of the fighting in the First World War (which was basically a massive military stalemate), victory was likely to go to the countries whose home front would hold firm the longest. The Russian home front was the first of the major warring powers to collapse. However, the Italian home front came close to collapsing, and eventual collapse in Austria and Germany was a significant factor in the events of 1918. The collapse came in Russia because large sections of the middle and upper classes, and the bulk of the organised workforce, were not as well integrated into the political order as in other countries. This was not to be the case for the Soviet government in the Second World War.

Why was the Russian home front so significant in the Russian war effort? On the home front, initial optimism soon gave way to concern and despair. There were supplies of food in Russia. But too often supplies did not get through, especially to cities, due to poor communications and the priority given to the military. This was particularly significant because the cities' populations swelled with extra workers, who were then increasingly deprived of basic necessities. Although there was support from allies, Russia had to rely essentially on its own efforts.

THE CRISIS OF THE REGIME

Difficulties on the home front coincided with what was widely seen as a failure of government. Attempts to reform the taxation and administrative systems failed. Additionally, the government depleted its own revenues by banning the production and sale of alcohol early in the war, which deprived it of an important source of taxation. More efficient taxes such as income tax were introduced too late. The government's traditional remedies of borrowing more and printing money led to rapid inflation and a decline in living standards.

Economic and financial problems and military failures destroyed the unity of the ruling group displayed in 1914. Nicholas caused exasperation by his growing reliance on his wife and Rasputin, his frequently unimaginative choice of ministers, and his decision to take charge of the army in 1915. The *duma* had initially rallied to the regime, but by 1915 was already (in the form of the Progressive Bloc) dominated by liberals calling for a government based on more popular support.

The tsar refused to listen to advice. As a result, he steadily lost the support of both politicians and those members of the upper class, liberals and intelligentsia who had felt excluded from influence before the war. The tsar and his entourage were increasingly seen as obstacles to success – hence his lack of support when the crisis suddenly erupted in 1917. However, it was not a case of Nicholas II simply leading Russia blindly into disaster. Throughout the war he felt committed to the **Anglo–French alliance** and ruled out the possibility of any separate peace with Germany – a peace that, in any case, would have been political suicide for his regime. This was not to be a problem for the Bolsheviks when they made huge concessions to the Germans in the Treaty of Brest-Litovsk in March 1918, since in their situation they had little to lose anyway.

Many historians have focused on the obvious weaknesses and apparent contradictions within the tsarist regime even before 1914. Additionally, the issue of how stable Russia was in 1914 was discussed on pages 52–3. However, there were specific developments during the war itself that contributed to the fall of the regime in 1917.

KEY EVENT

Anglo–French alliance The alliance had its origins in agreements made between France and Britain in 1904 – the Entente Cordiale. This in turn followed on from the Franco-Russian alliance of 1894, and was followed by agreements between Russia and Britain in 1907. Although these agreements were not military alliances, they became so when war began in 1914.

The erosion of tsarist authority. In the context of Russia's overall performance, this was something that happened gradually and cumulatively. The tsar certainly had to take some of the blame. The issue of Rasputin's influence is a case in point. The imperial family's involvement with Rasputin was very harmful to its reputation, yet there has been a tendency for historians to downplay his influence. Indeed, revisionists have sought to paint him in a more sympathetic light. They point out, for example, that his advice was sometimes better than that of the tsar's official advisers, and that Rasputin himself was not responsible for anybody's death, despite his colourful career. However, the fact remains that his activities were a major blow to the tsar's prestige and many of the tsar's former supporters were less prepared to stand by him in 1917 as a result.

Militancy in the working class. The organised section of the working class became more militant, and those who opposed the war gained support at the expense of those 'defencists' who followed the official line of supporting the war. However, even the defencists became opposed to the way in which the regime conducted the war. An increasing debate among historians, both inside and outside Russia, has included the following questions.

- What were the relative strengths of the 'radical' and 'defencist' factions?
- What proportion of the working class was actually 'organised'?
- What influence did radical and revolutionary political movements like the Bolsheviks have among the working class?

Change of character of the army. The army changed in character during the war. It has long been recognised that growing war weariness and declining morale were important factors in reducing the effectiveness of the Russian fighting man as the war dragged on unsuccessfully. But relatively little attention was paid to the officer class. This had been loyal in 1905. However, during the war, officers were increasingly recruited from the urban middle classes. These men often remained loyal to the concept of continued fighting, but like many influential people in civilian life, increasingly came to regard Nicholas II as an obstacle to success.

CONCLUSION

The First World War was clearly a catastrophic event both for the tsarist regime and for Russia as a whole. There is no argument about the fact that defeat and the privations caused by war were major factors in creating a situation in which discontent could build up and then erupt as it was to do in 1917. Other issues are more open to debate, such as the extent to which the influence of revolutionary parties was growing and the extent to which discontent was essentially spontaneous or organised.

The regime clearly bore some responsibility for the disasters, notably the tsar's handling of the government. However, it would be simplistic to accuse the regime of total incompetence. As with the other major powers, when the nature of the war became clear the regime was able, relatively quickly, to concentrate industrial production (including that necessary for defence) and to set up administrative controls.

The expansion of state control was not ultimately successful, but the efforts made did not suggest a totally incompetent regime. By 1916, the state was controlling most aspects of transport, industry and the distribution of food and fuel. It began to requisition necessary supplies in a way normally associated with the post-1917 communist regimes of Lenin and Stalin. Even many liberals supported these measures, as they also did, for example, in wartime Britain.

Unfortunately for the regime, increasing difficulties in the conduct of such a major war, the lack of military success and dissatisfaction with an increasingly isolated leadership at the top negated the effectiveness of other measures and created a climate in which some sort of revolutionary action was increasingly likely. To what extent that action would be spontaneous or the result of an organised coup was a very different matter.

6 Why were there two revolutions in Russia in 1917?

BACKGROUND

The events of the February/March revolution in Russia are well known and indisputable. Disturbances in Petrograd spiralled out of control. The tsar, away at the front and lacking support, abdicated. A Provisional Government was set up, dominated first by liberals and, from April 1917, by an uneasy coalition of liberals and moderate socialists. Significantly, the Bolsheviks did not join the coalition, and were thereby able to appear untainted by later difficulties that beset the government.

After the February revolution a *Soviet* was established in Petrograd. Historians commonly talk of 'dual power' in the months after February, with the Provisional Government and the *Soviet* in uneasy alliance. The reality was a collapse of state power, since the government had neither the authority nor coherent ideology underpinning it to immediately assume all the political and administrative functions of the old tsarist state. Meanwhile the *Soviet*, for all the claims of Soviet historians, had a limited power base and was not equipped for government.

There was therefore a power vacuum from the start with no centre of power, although several organisations and individuals – for example, Pavel Miliukov, Kerensky, Victor Chernov, and later Lenin and Kornilov – tried to impose a particular direction on events. With hindsight, it is clear that February 1917 was only the start of a revolutionary process.

The Provisional Government could not foresee this at the time, and had to deal with immediate priorities. It saw one of the first priorities as continuing the war against the Central Powers. It wasn't long before the government faced a number of difficulties that steadily eroded the optimism of the early weeks of the revolution and led to a decline in whatever authority it aspired to. Within a few months of its formation, the Provisional Government was toppled by a Bolshevik-led coup, which led to the formation of the Soviet state. In retrospect, too much was expected from the Provisional Government, particularly when Russia was consumed by war.

Interpretations of the two revolutions of 1917 were coloured by several factors. One such factor was the availability of Russian documentary evidence from the years of communist rule. Indeed, it wasn't until after the break-up of the Soviet Union in 1991 that many of the Soviet archives were opened. Some of the information made available at that time led to reinterpretations of events and personalities. For example, more evidence was made available of Lenin's ruthless approach to opposition immediately after the October revolution. Another important factor has been the influence of different ideological perspectives of historians and commentators, many of whom lived through these and subsequent events.

The orthodox Soviet interpretation of the events of 1917, unchallengeable while the USSR existed, was that Bolshevik influence was already important in creating the climate of popular discontent that made the February revolution possible. The working classes in cities such as Petrograd and Moscow were increasingly organised and class conscious. Although the Bolshevik Party initially supported the February revolution and the creation of the Provisional Government, the return of Lenin to Russia in April 1917 enabled the Bolsheviks to realise the error of this approach.

Lenin made them realise that, despite having fulfilled a valuable function in overthrowing tsarism, the new regime was only a temporary phase that served the interests of the middle classes but was a betrayal of those of the working class. He also helped the Communist Party to realise that its true duty was to work towards overthrowing the Provisional Government as soon as possible, regardless of the state of economic development in Russia, which did not necessarily meet the 'orthodox' Marxist criteria of economic development.

Nevertheless, the orthodox Soviet school, while recognising the important contribution of Lenin and the Communist Party organisation as the vanguard of the working class, also insisted that the October revolution was a popular revolution of the masses. It was an inevitable consequence that would have happened even without the First World War and whether the tsarist regime had attempted reforms or not.

The Soviet school of historiography tried to reconcile two potentially contradictory positions. On the one hand it emphasised the importance of fundamental change arising out of class conflict and denied the importance of particular individuals in influencing history. On the other, it simultaneously praised (and indeed magnified) the contribution of selected individuals, notably Lenin, whose status after death was virtually raised to that of sainthood.

This official Soviet interpretation was only challenged within Russia from the mid-1980s, when Gorbachev's policy of *glasnost* allowed a reassessment of these events. This 'revisionist' approach led to some Russian historians adopting a more sympathetic approach to Nicholas II and the many problems his regime faced both before and during the First World War.

THE DEBATE ABOUT THE FEBRUARY 1917 REVOLUTION

The historiographical debate about 1917 was always more intense outside Russia between 1917 and 1991. This debate has been divided into two schools of thought – the liberal, or optimistic, school and the pessimist school.

The liberal, or optimistic, school

This was a group of western historians, influenced in most cases by their own beliefs in the virtues of western liberal democracy, with its emphasis on the rights of the individual as opposed to the primacy of the state.

Their interpretation suggested that, for all its faults, the tsarist regime showed itself to be capable of reform before 1914, and might well have survived but for the First World War. The February revolution was spontaneous. Revolutionary groups like the Bolsheviks played an insignificant role.

The pessimist school

This was a group of western historians who, while not necessarily sympathetic to Soviet interpretations, argued against the view that the tsarist regime was capable of the sort of reform that might have saved Russia from revolution. The reforms that were attempted – for example, Stolypin's agrarian reforms – were limited in their effects.

The fundamental difference between this school and Soviet historians was that most western historians, unless Marxists themselves, did not believe that the fall of tsarism automatically had to lead to a communist revolution. Indeed, many outcomes were possible, ranging from a left-wing coup to a right-wing military dictatorship.

Different shades of interpretation

In the light of more recent evidence, there have been some different shades of interpretation since the mid-1980s, often classified as revisionism.

In the West, some social historians paid less attention to the activities of politicians and political structures, and more to social developments which had tended to receive less treatment previously. One of the earliest examples of this school of thought came in S. Smith's book *Red Petrograd*. This book follows the growth of revolutionary feeling among factory workers even before 1914, a feeling fuelled as much by political sentiment as by dissatisfaction with economic conditions. There was subsequently a vigorous debate about the extent to which these feelings were exploited by organised political groups such as the Bolsheviks and Mensheviks.

While there has never been an agreed interpretation of the events of 1917, the work of 'social historians' has been important in helping to create a more multidimensional view of events by demonstrating that what happened in the lives of ordinary people was as significant as the actions of important political figures.

PERSONALITIES

Despite the Soviet insistence that class struggle based on economic and historical forces ultimately determined the fate of societies, personalities were clearly important in the events of 1917 – particularly between the two revolutions.

History is often very unsympathetic to the losers. As leader of the Socialist Revolutionaries (SR), the largest revolutionary party, Victor Chernov should have been a key figure in 1917. But he conspicuously lacked Lenin's sense of political timing and was hesitant at key moments. Joining the Provisional Government is frequently seen as a major error on his part, although Chernov himself was to be very critical of his role in the split between the left and right SRs, which weakened his party.

Two of the key figures in 1917 were Kerensky and Lenin

Kerensky

Interpretations of Kerensky have been very varied. He was described by Lenin as a 'democratic windbag'. Yet, in 1917, the British ambassador to Russia called him 'the most influential member of the government'.

Criticisms of Kerensky tend to focus on his attempts to be above party, and maintain influence both with the *Soviet* and the government. This has been seen as weakness and indecision, but until after the July crisis, Kerensky enjoyed great popularity in Russia, reinforced by his charismatic speechmaking. While his reluctance to be committed to one party (even his own – the SRs) was possibly a weakness later, his non-partisan approach was much commended at the time. His reputation suffered a remarkable turnaround after the failure of the June offensive and the growing dissatisfaction with the coalition government. He was also discredited by the Kornilov Revolt.

Kerensky's personal cult attracted criticism and he was ultimately defeated. Historically, his reputation plummeted because the crisis that gripped Russia was increasingly ascribed to him, and his critics were on both the left and the right. His reputation was not helped by his own self-justifying memoirs. But to some extent he was made a scapegoat for other failings as well as his own.

Lenin

This is not the place to discuss interpretations of Lenin at length, but his role in 1917 should be considered.

Often he was not at the centre of events. He returned to Russia from exile as recently as April 1917, and even then was frequently in hiding before the October revolution. But it is difficult to imagine the Bolshevik success without his presence, despite Trotsky's contribution to the seizure and maintenance of power (a fact recognised by the demonisation of Lenin by partisan historians on the right). More balanced interpretations of Lenin's role include that of Robert Service, who has emphasised some key features applicable to 1917.

- Lenin had confidence in his policies and his own leadership, which enabled him, for example, to take on opponents within his own party after April.
- Despite his considerable theorising, Lenin was also a very practical and flexible politician. He seized the moment. In April 1917, he sensed that counter-revolution might triumph if socialists did not act. Consequently, he threw himself wholeheartedly into preparing for revolution, despite the misgivings of many Marxists about the state of Russia's development.

THE OCTOBER REVOLUTION

Interpretations of the events leading to the Bolshevik take-over of power in October 1917 have long been characterised by vigorous debate, often influenced by ideological preconceptions. The evidence itself is constantly being added to by new material from the archives.

The main interpretations of October can be summarised as follows.

The 'official' Soviet view from 1918 to the mid-1980s

The February revolution was only a step in the revolutionary process which could not be completed until Russia became a socialist state as part of a European or world revolution. The following extract, from Y. Kukushkin, typifies this interpretation.

> *The February bourgeois-democratic revolution did not bring the working masses of Russia either liberation from the domination of their exploiters, or Russia's withdrawal from the imperialist war ... The counter-revolutionaries installed a bourgeois-landowner Provisional Government ... The struggle over the issue of war and peace graphically demonstrated the anti-popular essence of the Provisional Government* (Kukushkin, *History of the USSR: An Outline of Socialist Construction*).

While the process of a second revolution was inevitable – it 'lay in the logic of history' – the Bolsheviks played an important role in influencing the precise timing of events.

The October revolution was essentially a popular rising by workers and peasants, but their activities were guided by the Bolsheviks under the leadership of Lenin, who argued successfully against the more cautious approach of leading colleagues such as Kamenev and Zinoviev. They claimed that the Bolsheviks did not yet have sufficient mass support. Lenin outmanoeuvred other groups such as the Mensheviks who were essentially waiting for events to happen rather than leading them. Despite the important role of Trotsky in the *Soviet* and his role in the Bolshevik *coup*, his contribution was written out of Soviet history after his fall from grace and exile from the USSR in the mid-1920s.

Post-communist Russian interpretations

Russian historians in the post-communist period from the late-1980s onwards continued to recognise the significance of Lenin's leadership. However, they were far more critical of the actual process of the coup, tending to agree with the western liberal view that it was carried out by a small but well organised group that did not represent the interests of the majority of Russians.

The liberal school

The mainstream of western historical thought in the decades after the revolution was as follows.

October 1917 was a coup carried out by a small group, well organised and daring, but successful only because the Provisional Government had lost all authority, there was a power vacuum and no other group had the organisation or will to stop the Bolsheviks. The seizure of power was the relatively easy part – in fact, it was almost bloodless. The real struggle would begin when the enemies of the Bolsheviks finally woke up to what was happening and reacted against this unrepresentative group, resulting in civil war in 1918. This view became accepted by many post-Soviet Russian historians from the 1990s onwards.

A minority of western historians – sometimes misleadingly called revisionists, sometimes called libertarians – had always put a different gloss on this interpretation. These were writers of a left-wing but anti-communist persuasion who believed that the struggle in Russia was essentially between workers fighting for their freedom and an authoritarian Bolshevik Party. They claimed that this party hijacked the struggle of the working class to throw off the shackles of one authoritarian regime (tsarism) and replaced it with another, and ultimately more efficient controlling authority, that of the monolithic communists.

This interpretation tends to focus on the fact that the workers were not a unified group but a mass of individuals or small groups, often with specific economic aims but with no coherent political view. Because they were not organised, they were in no position to prevent an organised coup by a political group claiming to act in their name.

Other historians have emphasised that the Bolsheviks themselves were hardly a monolithic, closely organised group. Even in April 1917, Lenin had difficulty in imposing the arguments of the April Theses on some sections of the Communist Party. Many of the new recruits to the Communist Party in the revolutionary months of 1917 had their own agenda. Some were recruits from other groups such as the Mensheviks and the Socialist Revolutionaries, and were not as closely organised as was presented in Soviet and much western historiography. Much of the consolidation of authority within the Communist Party occurred during the subsequent civil war when the Bolsheviks were fighting for their lives.

WAS THE OCTOBER REVOLUTION A COUP?

Most western historians and post-Soviet Russian historians have argued that the October revolution was essentially a coup organised and carried out by a relatively small group, taking advantage of a fluid political situation. Typical of left-wing interpretations of the revolution is the quotation below from A. Woods.

Arguments for the claim that the October revolution was a coup
- Relatively few people took part in the seizure of power, which was essentially bloodless in Petrograd.
- Power was seized by an organised party, not the mass of the working class.
- The seizure of power was remarkably smooth – the government virtually collapsed without a fight.

Arguments against the claim that the October revolution was a coup
- Left-wing historians would claim that, during the previous nine months, the Bolsheviks had won considerable support from workers and even many peasants, and the Red Guards who seized the Winter Palace were only the tip of an iceberg. The argument that there was no real revolution 'confuses the armed insurrection with the revolution, that is to say, it confuses the part with the whole. In reality, the insurrection is only a part of the revolution … nine-tenths of the tasks were already accomplished beforehand, by winning over the decisive majority of workers and soldiers' (Woods, *Bolshevism: The Road To Revolution*).
- The Bolsheviks were a relatively small group, but represented the interests of a much larger number of workers. This was essentially Lenin's own argument.

CONCLUSION

There is a danger in attaching labels to schools of historical interpretation. Phrases like 'the liberal interpretation' or 'revisionism' can become artificial constructs that adapt facts to fit preconceived theories. Nevertheless, the debate over interpretations of the 1917 revolutions is a real and vibrant one, and is constantly added to as new material comes to light.

All interpretations have their value as well as their limitations. Few historians inside or outside of Russia would accept the pre-1985 orthodox communist line that the October revolution was a popular rising led, but not controlled, by the Bolshevik Party, whatever evidence there is that Bolshevik influence was strong in particular factory districts.

The so-called liberal school has highlighted the important roles of Lenin and Trotsky, and played down the role of popular support. But in some cases, it has exaggerated the notion of an anti-democratic coup against democratic values – an interpretation that is possibly over-sympathetic to the Provisional Government and misunderstands the chaotic nature of Russia at this time.

Other interpretations, such as the libertarian school outlined on pages 64–5, are controversial and their validity is sometimes undermined by selective use of evidence. None the less, they do have value in reminding us to look at a wider range of sources – for example, what was happening in the factories and workshops of Petrograd. They also take account of a wide range of social and economic factors rather than focusing just on major political events and the activities of prominent politicians and activists like Kerensky and Lenin.

The truth almost certainly lies somewhere between all these interpretations. The year 1917 saw two revolutions, the first more spontaneous than the other. Undoubtedly the second was a coup led by a relatively small group. The real argument is about the amount of support that group had, and the extent to which the initial success was due more to the disunity of the Bolsheviks' opponents than to the strength of the Bolsheviks themselves. The key facts about October 1917 are probably as follows.

- The Provisional Government was probably fatally weakened before October 1917. It was perhaps not a case of the Bolsheviks or the Provisional Government, but more which political structure would replace the government. It could have been one of the right or the left, and different shades of either. The Bolshevik victory was not inevitable, whatever degree of support the Bolsheviks had on the ground. But at that particular time and in that particular place – the Russian capital –

they seized the initiative in a power vacuum. And, at a time of national crisis, an extremist group – whether from the left or right – was always going to have the advantage over moderates.

- The actual take-over of power was significant, although it was only the beginning of far more momentous events. The storming of the Winter Palace was of great symbolic and propaganda importance, but only that. The real struggle for power was to come. Even when it appeared to be over by 1921, in the Bolsheviks' favour, Russia had not changed significantly. Despite the overthrow of tsarism, and the creation of a Soviet state and a number of important decrees (for example, those on land ownership and the ending of discrimination based on gender), many of the fundamentals of Russian society had not changed. Taking a longer-term perspective, although 1917 was the necessary precondition, the really significant revolution was that of Stalin in the late 1920s and 1930s. This produced a far more important economic and social transformation of the USSR, and determined its main characteristics for the next 50 years – in fact almost up to the break-up of the communist state in the late-1980s.

7 How and why did Lenin succeed in staying in power between 1917 and 1924?

THE ESTABLISHMENT OF SOVIET POWER

Lenin had no concerns about removing the freedoms the Provisional Government had granted after the February revolution. The Bolsheviks argued that the Provisional Government was only an instrument of bourgeois capitalism, opposed to the interests of the working class. Therefore it was legitimate to deprive owners of their land, banks and factories, in addition to the vote. The creation of the one-party state was also high on Lenin's agenda. Proof of his ruthless, pragmatic approach was seen in two events that took place soon after the October revolution.

- The signing of an armistice with Germany, followed by the Treaty of Brest-Litovsk, which gave away huge areas of land and resources. It was necessary in order for the new regime to have peace and time to consolidate. In any case, Lenin expected a revolution in Germany which might lead to a restoration of Russia's losses.
- Dissolving the newly elected Constituent Assembly, because it failed to produce a Bolshevik majority.

The latter action in particular was interpreted by many western, anti-Soviet historians as evidence of the fundamentally totalitarian nature of Bolshevism. Born as a secretive, disciplined party, intolerant of dissent, the Bolshevik Party was hardly likely to change its nature on coming to power. In any case, the situation required ruthlessness and determination to survive.

Having seized power in a small area of Russia in 1917, the Bolsheviks were bound to face opposition from a range of opponents once these had woken up to the implications of the October coup. The Bolsheviks had a bitter struggle to survive. The civil war intensified authoritarian trends within the Communist Party, including the centralisation of the Communist Party structure itself, although there is some debate among historians as to whether these developments would have taken place even without a war.

ults of the
tions for the
stituent
embly, which
briefly in
8.

	Votes	Number of deputies	% of the vote
SRs	21.8 million	410	53%
Bolsheviks	10.0 million	175	24%
Kadets	2.1 million	17	5%
Mensheviks	1.4 million	18	3%
Others	6.3 million	62	15%

1919 Bolshevik
propaganda
poster, depicting
death to the
serpent of
imperialism.

THE NEW SOVIET STATE

The dissolution of the Constituent Assembly

When the elections to the Assembly (planned before the October revolution) were held in November 1917 on the principle of universal suffrage, the results were as shown in the table on page 69.

The results were a blow to Lenin, who promptly closed down the Assembly. This was apparently proof of his determination to stay in power and also of the Bolsheviks' contempt for 'bourgeois' democratic forms. The dissolution has been seized on by many historians as evidence of an early move towards the establishment of a one-party state.

Bolsheviks saw the events differently. In the elections they had done well in the larger industrial cities. Lenin claimed that these results represented the more 'advanced' sections of the working class, whose views should carry more weight than more 'backward' areas of Russia. On a broader level, it was also claimed that the Assembly was 'a cover for bourgeois revolution', and that in the confusion immediately following the October revolution, many Russians did not really understand for whom they were voting. Many historians have rejected this interpretation. Richard Pipes is representative of the unsympathetic interpretation of Bolshevik actions:

> The critical event in the political degeneration of the Bolshevik regime was the dispersal of the Constituent Assembly. If, as the Bolsheviks claimed in self-justification, the Assembly elected in November 1917 no longer reflected the mood of the masses as of January 1918, then they should have held fresh elections instead of liquidating it (Pipes, Russia Under the Bolshevik Regime).

Historians more sympathetic to Lenin's standpoint – for example, Marcel Liebmann – have been more inclined to accept the Bolshevik argument that factors such as the division within the SR movement since the elections nullified the result. Liebmann also argued that 'the industrial proletariat and the masses it led were against the Constituent Assembly and for the Soviets; the bourgeoisie and the conservative or reactionary elements were, on the contrary, against the Soviets and for the Constituent Assembly' (Liebmann, Leninism Under Lenin). This view legitimised or at least explained Lenin's actions in the context of the time.

The centralisation of power within the Communist Party

The Bolshevik Party was far from being a monolithic entity at the time of the revolution. Local branches of the Communist Party and local *soviets* exercised considerable initiative, particularly in a large country in which communications, never easy, had been further disrupted by war.

A 1919 Bolshevik poster caricaturing the evils of capitalism.

Historians such as Leonard Schapiro (*The Communist Party of the Soviet Union*) claim that centralisation in the hands of a Party elite was always high on the Bolshevik agenda. Other historians have paid less attention to centralising tendencies, looking not so much at central Party structures as other institutions like the *soviets*. These acted as instruments of local government, particularly from the summer of 1918 when old local government institutions such as the *zemstvos* and the *dumas* were abolished. Political groups such as the Mensheviks and SRs were expelled from the *soviets*, which were also responsible between 1918 and 1922 for mobilisation and conscription into the Red Army (among other functions). The nature of the *soviets* began to change, but the debate is about the extent to which this was intentional or accidental. Although the *soviets* began life as revolutionary mass bodies, they quickly became bureaucratic organs of local government under central control, and remained so for the next 70 years.

There is evidence that in the months after the revolution many village and city *soviets* were subject to the pull of 'local patriotism' and acted independently. In other cases they became almost defunct. But from 1919 there was considerable strengthening of control over the Communist Party by the central organisation.

Although local Party representatives were regularly sent to Party congresses, the more significant process was sending out representatives from the centre to gradually take control of local Party organisations, bringing them into line with the objectives of the central leadership. That leadership itself was concentrated initially in the Central Committee, but from 1919 in the *Politburo*. Administration was centralised in the *Orgburo* and the Secretariat.

The Party structure was democratic on paper, since each level of the Communist Party administration was supposed to represent the views of delegates from the organisation below. In practice, however, it was a 'top down' rather than a 'bottom up' model, since key decisions were handed down from above. Centralisation was certainly partly due to the civil war, which made such control and uniform decision making seem imperative, and many local Party members welcomed support from the centre. But was centralisation also inherent in the Communist Party philosophy and structure?

The Tenth Party Congress. The opportunity for dissent or free expression of individual opinion within the Communist Party was steadily eroded. A key moment was the Tenth Party Congress of 1921, which banned factions within the Communist Party. While the Decree on Party Unity did not stop disagreement among leading communists, it did effectively silence free debate at a lower level. Groups previously at odds with the leadership – notably the Democratic Centralists calling for less centralised control, and the Workers' Opposition group, which wanted less Party authority over workers in the factories – were silenced. Historians often see this measure as an inevitable step in the formalisation of communist control.

An 'Agitship' used to spread communist propaganda.

The significance of the date should be emphasised; 1921 was the year of the Kronstadt Revolt. Leaving aside the resistance to collectivisation a decade later, this revolt was the last expression of armed resistance to the communist regime by what had once been loyal supporters. Soon afterwards Lenin introduced the NEP. However, this economic relaxation was deliberately accompanied by the ban on factions to signify the fact that economic 'retreat' might be a necessity, but was to be accompanied by more centralisation and clampdown of dissent within the Communist Party, to ensure the dominance of the leadership.

There was certainly no indication of retreat here. In his new role of General Secretary, Stalin was able to use this decree to further discipline the Communist Party membership. Later, he used the ban on factions to help him overcome rivals for the leadership after Lenin's death.

Although historians still debate the exact role of the *soviets* and the degree to which there was any 'democracy' in the western liberal tradition, there is now a general consensus that the channels of power developed as follows in the two years or so after the revolution. At first the *soviets* were more important than the Communist Party in day-to-day administration, but the Communist Party gradually began to exercise power through the *soviets*, particularly under Yakov Sverdlov, who controlled both the Communist Party apparatus and was Chairman of the Central Executive Committee of Soviets until his death in March 1919. From 1919, the Communist Party was increasingly the dominant force, controlling all key appointments, so that *soviets* had only administrative functions.

There is a key debate about how monolithic the Communist Party actually was both at this time and later under Stalin.

The abolition of other parties and the establishment of the one-party state

The Bolsheviks' intentions may have seemed clear from the start, as seen in their treatment of the Constituent Assembly. However, while 'bourgeois' parties like the Kadets were banned early on, other left-wing parties were allowed to co-exist briefly, albeit they were increasingly harassed, finding it difficult, for example, to publish their newspapers.

The Left Socialist Revolutionaries had limited influence. In 1921, all other parties were banned and only the Communist Party (the official title of the Bolsheviks from March 1918) existed. Persecution of other parties was now formalised and by 1922 they had ceased to exist as formal structures. The one-party state was complete. Indeed, it was not until the late 1980s that other political parties were allowed to form and challenge the Communist Party for supremacy.

A communist poster from the early 1920s. The Menshevik and the Socialist Revolutionary try in vain to hold back the forward march of the determined worker.

However, the notion that Lenin established a monolithic Party almost overnight can no longer be defended. Although the Communist Party was loyal to the leadership of Lenin (as historians like Robert Service have shown), there were limits to the degree of centralisation and hierarchical power. Despite the prevailing ideology, there was still dissension and factionalism within the Communist Party. It was a dynamic as well as a bureaucratic Party. That is why there were to be periodic purges by the leadership. It also explains why Stalin destroyed the old party leadership in the 1930s. He understood that not everyone in the Communist Party would always follow the leadership. Even Lenin found this before and after the revolution, when he had difficulty in persuading colleagues to follow his changes of policy.

Opposition from within the Communist Party to directives from the top was to be a recurring theme in Soviet history, although in the last decades of Soviet rule the opposition was more likely to come as a result of conservative reluctance to change rather than from deep-seated ideological disagreements over policy.

The establishment of Party control over the state

Although Russia was in chaos at the time of the Bolshevik take-over in 1917, it gave one considerable advantage to Lenin. He did not have to take account of the traditional structures of government and administration (which he despised in any case), and was instead free to create new forms. In this respect, Russia was in a fundamentally different situation from, for example, Germany at the time of the Nazi take-over in 1933, when existing forms of administration continued to exist alongside Nazi organisations.

The Bolsheviks created the Central Executive Committee, elected by the All-Russian Congress of Soviets. This body was elected by members of local *soviets* and had the responsibility of passing laws. However, in practice this meant rubber stamping decrees already decided by the higher organs of the Communist Party – principally the *Politburo*.

Above the Central Executive Committee was *Sovnarkom*, the Council of People's Commissars, which in theory directed policy. This dual system of state and Party institutions lasted as long as the USSR itself, but from the beginning the Communist Party institutions had much more power. Leading communists belonged to both state and Party organisations at the highest level.

The Soviet constitution of 1923, which replaced that of 1918, contained a strong element of fiction. The new constitution created a federal state, the Union of Soviet Socialist Republics (USSR), in which each republic had equal rights, including that of secession. This right was never exercised. Soviet historians interpreted this constitution as evidence of 'the practical realisation of Lenin's ideas of harmonising the principles of consolidating the state unity of the constituent republics with the provision of comprehensive guarantees of their sovereign rights' (Kukushkin, *History of the USSR*). The reality was that power was centralised in Moscow, increasingly so, and this emphasised the fact that it was the Communist Party that controlled the USSR rather than formal state structures.

Government by coercion

Another true indication of where power lay was the fact that the secret police was directly responsible to Party organs, not the state. The *Cheka*, set up soon after the revolution, was the instrument for eliminating all potential or real opposition to the regime. Replaced by the **OGPU** (in 1923), the **NKVD** (in 1934) and eventually the **KGB**, the political police eventually had its arbitrary powers restricted as recently as the 1960s onwards.

For many years after Lenin's death, historians argued about his responsibility for the terror that was part of Soviet rule in the years after the revolution. In the period of the NEP, the arbitrary use of terror considerably declined, to return with a vengeance under Stalin. Under Stalin's successors, the USSR remained a police state, but less arbitrary in its approach. Citizens who conformed were safe from persecution, although dissidents were liable to severe treatment.

Many historians argued that Lenin was less ruthless than Stalin. While accepting that there was a Red Terror during the civil war, it was often claimed that this was largely due to the desperation of the Bolshevik position during this period when the regime was fighting for its existence against equally ruthless enemies, and that terror was not something that was necessarily inherent or inevitable in the Soviet regime. Attempts were frequently made to distinguish Lenin's rule from that of Stalin, who took over a USSR that seemed more secure from its enemies, and therefore was in a situation in which there seemed less excuse for arbitrary use of terror.

The emphasis has changed in recent years. Evidence released after the collapse of the USSR increasingly showed Lenin's willingness, and indeed insistence, on using terror as a legitimate instrument of government, and his personal involvement in campaigns against groups such as the Mensheviks.

HOW DID THE BOLSHEVIKS WIN THE CIVIL WAR?

The civil war of 1918–21 was crucial in securing Soviet rule. Defeat would have meant the destruction of the Communist Party and the establishment of probably some sort of right-wing quasi-military regime, since the restoration of the monarchy was not an option for most Russians.

Most historians now accept that the Reds had many advantages in the civil war, including the unified leadership of the communists under Lenin, whose leadership was unchallenged, and the skill and determination of Trotsky in creating and leading the Red Army. Another advantage was the control by the communists of industrial centres, areas of concentrated population and interior lines of communication. The 'policy' of War Communism also helped their cause.

In contrast, the Whites, comprising various opponents of the Bolsheviks or Reds, appeared to suffer several disadvantages. There was a lack of a unified command or strategy leading to uncoordinated attacks and a lack of support from ordinary Russians who had no wish to give up their recently acquired land. Furthermore, the aid from foreign armies of intervention was largely ineffectual.

There is always a danger of interpretations being coloured by hindsight. But where there is disagreement among historians, it is often about the relative weight that should be given to Red 'advantages' and White 'disadvantages'. Francesco Benvenuti (*The Bolsheviks and the Red Army 1918–1922*) showed how, for all Trotsky's much-lauded skills, he faced opposition not just from within the Communist Party but also from some of the high command of the Red Army itself, which felt that he did not represent its interests sufficiently strongly. Evan Mawdsley (*The Russian Civil War*) emphasises many of the Reds' advantages in the war, while arguing that the personal contributions of Lenin and Trotsky should not be overrated. He also dispelled the traditional view of the White armies as being essentially class based, showing that many of the soldiers were of non-noble status.

Historians now pay more attention to those who did *not* fight for the Reds or Whites. Geoffrey Swain (*Russia's Civil War*), for example, described the 'unknown civil war' or the 'three-cornered fight' involving not just Reds and Whites but also the peasant armies or 'Greens'. These were generally led by anarchists or SRs, and they came far closer to success than is usually acknowledged, especially in Soviet historiography that focused on the Whites or 'class enemies' of the Bolsheviks.

Peasants were more prepared in the last resort to tolerate the Reds rather than the Whites, because the latter were not prepared to compromise on the issue of land ownership. However, the resistance of the peasantry to

A Bolshevik propaganda poster from the civil war. Generals Denikin and Yudenich are throttled by the hands of the Dictatorship of the Proletariat.

grain requisitioning by the Reds played a major influence in later Bolshevik policy towards the peasants. Those like Stalin who faced peasant resistance during the civil war did not forget the experience, which influenced attitudes towards the peasants in the period of collectivisation of the late 1920s.

This continuity of experience led historian Andrea Graziosi to take a longer-term perspective. He described the civil war of 1918–21 as ending in a stalemate between Reds and Greens, one episode in what he called, during the period from 1917 to 1933, the 'great Soviet peasant war'.

Other historians like Christopher Read (*From Tsar To Soviets*) have been critical of interpretations of the civil war as being a decisive force in shaping the Soviet system. While some commentators have written about the influence of the war in hardening attitudes within the Communist Party, militarising it and making it more ready to adopt harsher policies in future years, Read argued that centralisation of authority and an authoritarian approach were inherent in Bolshevik ideology. They would have been key features even if the civil war had not occurred.

The core of Bolshevism was its commitment to class warfare. In any case, Mawdsley argued that there was no real distinction between revolution and civil war, in that in the context of these years there could not be one without the other. The Bolsheviks seized power, and so as a minority force they were bound to face opposition from opponents who saw no valid reason for accepting the coup as a legitimate political outcome.

WAR COMMUNISM AND THE NEW ECONOMIC POLICY

The communist regime instituted a number of drastic economic measures to sustain the war effort in the civil war years. These included nationalisation, militarisation of industry to ensure that priority was given to war production and, perhaps most controversially, a ruthless policy of requisitioning food from the peasantry to ensure that industrial workers and the Red Army were fed.

The phrase 'War Communism' is really a misnomer. It was invented by Lenin in 1921 at the time when the NEP was being introduced. The phrase is also confusing because it has been used in different ways – for example, to describe the drastic economic measures adopted by the regime during this period, or to describe a particular mentality of 'struggle' that pervaded this and later periods, and even to describe the economic organisation later adopted by Stalin.

War Communism is sometimes seen as a co-ordinated policy, when in fact the measures introduced were largely improvised and applied at various times during this period. Pressures from below forced nationalisation to go at a faster pace than the leadership originally intended. There was bound to be a clash between the utopianism of many Bolsheviks and the practical needs of the situation.

Interpretations have also been coloured by the ideological gloss given to these measures at the time and later. To ardent communists like Bukharin, the measures were welcome evidence that Russia was taking decisive steps on the road to creating socialism. Hence, for example, the fact that rampant inflation (with money losing its value and in many cases replaced by barter as a means of exchange) was welcomed as proof that the mechanisms of capitalism were already redundant.

Others have dwelt far less on the ideological gloss and have concentrated on the fact that War Communism was essentially a pragmatic response to an emergency situation. As economic historians like Silvana Malle showed (*The Economic Organisation of War Communism 1918–1921*), there was little coherence to the measures. Co-ordinated and centralised control of supply and distribution was achieved only in military production. Rational planning was further complicated by the lack of economic indicators to replace traditional market indicators.

One Soviet historian admitted that War Communism 'was, of course, a forced measure resulting from the extraordinarily difficult situation in Russia at that time. "War communism" is not an economically inevitable stage in the development of a socialist revolution' (Kukushkin, *History of the USSR*).

Lenin himself gave different interpretations of the measures taken by his regime during these years. When it was clear by 1921 that War Communism was creating major discontent (especially among the peasantry, who regarded requisitioning as state-sponsored theft) and industrial production was falling, he decided to change the policy. The signs of a dangerous backlash against the policy were already present, so Lenin had decided on the NEP before the Kronstadt Revolt. This has sometimes been taken as the ultimate symbol of discontent against the new communist regime, partly because Lenin himself referred to Kronstadt as an event that 'lit up reality like a flash of lightning'.

The NEP, with its emphasis on economic co-operation rather than coercion, its tolerance of private enterprise, and in particular the granting to peasants of the right to pay tax and keep their food supplies, marked a period of economic recovery. However, it is difficult to determine the extent to which this recovery was due to the NEP, and the extent to which it was due to the ending of the civil war and the consolidation of communist rule. Almost certainly it was a combination of both.

Lenin did not have a consistent view on the NEP. At various times he referred to it as a measure introduced entirely for pragmatic reasons, to end the dissatisfaction of the peasantry and ensure that the communists remained in power. At other times he gave it a firmer ideological justification, arguing that NEP was a logical step in the advance towards socialism – a form of state capitalism, a half-way house between capitalism and a socialist society in which private ownership would disappear.

Lenin's most realistic evaluation of War Communism and the reason for change was his statement that the communists had been 'carried away by a wave of enthusiasm ... We thought that by direct orders of the proletarian state, we could organise state production and distribution of products communistically in a land of petty peasants'. Lenin was recognising the fact that the peasant mentality did not fit in with his conception of socialism. A popular Soviet textbook of 1934 justified the changes in policy as follows:

> War Communism fully justified itself in conditions of civil war. But it would have been a mistake to insist on a continuance of the policy of War Communism after those circumstances had disappeared which had necessitated it. The New Economic Policy did not flow only from the peculiar national features of Russia. NEP is the normal economic policy of the proletariat after revolution.

These debates were not just an ideological gloss. All communists, including Lenin, believed that socialism was the ultimate goal. The disagreements were about the pace of change and at what stage the process of achieving socialism through industrialisation could be achieved, particularly if the anticipated spread of revolution around the world did not materialise and the USSR were left isolated.

This did not stop strong disagreements among communists themselves. Many of these were highly critical of the NEP and its apparent compromise with private enterprise, which permitted the growth of a class of entrepreneurs and wealthy peasants who were able to make profits at the expense of others.

A SOCIAL AND CULTURAL REVOLUTION?

The communists were not interested just in economic change. There was enthusiasm for bringing about a genuine social and cultural revolution. After all, Marxists referred to cultural and social factors as part of the superstructure of society that overlay the economic base, the dictatorship of the proletariat. Early Soviet measures revealed a mixture of idealism and ruthlessness characteristic of this period.

The Church. The Bolsheviks were bound to oppose the authority of the Orthodox Church as one of the traditional pillars of support of the tsarist regime, and a competing ideological force. Hence they carried out drastic measures such as the nationalisation of Church property. However, as a pragmatic recognition of the hold the Church still had over ordinary people (especially in the countryside), worship was still allowed, although discouraged. Brutal attacks on Church personnel and property in the early months of the civil war had failed to destroy it as an institution.

The problem of Church–state relations was to persist throughout Soviet history. Soviet historians painted the Church as leading the forces of counter-revolution against the communists. However, there is now more recognition of the fact that the hierarchy of the Church generally adopted a neutral or even conciliatory position once it realised early on that the communist regime seemed likely to stay.

Until the 1960s there were periodic bouts of persecution and tolerance. Less tolerated than the Orthodox Church were religious groups that sought to overtly evangelise and gain converts. In republics with a predominantly Muslim population, the Bolsheviks were initially cautious, since religion was so bound up with everyday life. Under Stalin the approach hardened, with attempts to 'russify' the population and create 'Soviet man', free from all ideologies that competed with the official communist one. But this was never completely successful.

A legitimate criticism of western historiography is that the importance of the Orthodox Church in Russia has been underestimated. Even though it was already in a state of internal crisis at the time of the revolution and faced considerable anti-clerical feeling, the Church continued to maintain a hold on sections of the population.

Social equality. At first, women appeared to gain considerably from the Bolshevik revolution. They were granted social equality and greater freedoms to get divorce and abortion. These gains were largely illusory. Women remained essentially second class citizens, particularly in Muslim areas. Most tellingly, women did not have an impressive record of promotion within the ranks of the Communist Party itself.

Too often, historians have treated women as a cohesive group, when in reality the revolution had a very different impact on different groups. Over 50 per cent of female recruits to the Communist Party between 1917 and 1921 came from the middle and upper ranks of society. Some 37 per cent were proletarians, and only 5 per cent peasants. Female peasants were not won over by the revolution, and were to play a major part in the resistance to collectivisation in the late 1920s.

Women in the cities were far more affected by the Bolshevik revolution, although greater access to education and employment was counterbalanced by their continued domestic responsibilities and traditional male assumptions.

The fate of particular social groups depended largely on how they were viewed by the new regime. The 'bourgeoisie', a term conveniently used to include not just property owners, businessmen and other representatives of capitalist society, but anyone with whom the communists disagreed, lost not only their property but also other privileges or rights. For example, only 'socially useful' citizens retained the right to vote.

Cultural revolution. Lenin was a cultural conservative. He did accept that proletarian culture would look very different from the 'traditional' Russian culture that he himself enjoyed. However, he believed that attitudes could not be changed overnight.

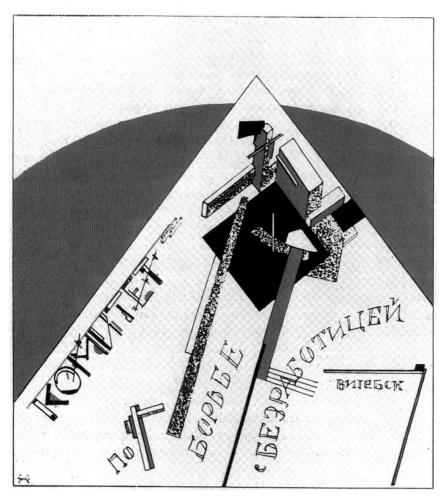

Lazar Lissitzky's 1919 cover design for the book *The Committee for Fighting Unemployment.*

New forms of cultural expression were enthusiastically embraced – notably the cinema, which had great propaganda potential. Many artists, writers and musicians, by no means all communists, carried out their own revolution in the arts, although often building on movements already taking place before 1917. However, many intellectuals were not communists. Experimentation in the arts was not just the preserve of enthusiasts like Vladimir Mayakovsky who eagerly embraced new 'proletarian' forms.

Compared with the Stalinist era, Lenin's regime was relatively tolerant of individual cultural expression. It was still possible to create works of art and literature that were not overtly political. However, political expression was strictly censored.

The effects of cultural change have been debated at length. To what extent was there a new proletarian ideology? The experimental political films of Sergei Eisenstein have been widely admired for their innovative techniques, especially in the West. However, some evidence suggests that ordinary Russians much preferred Hollywood films. Under Stalin they were to have no choice.

Some cultural historians – for example, James von Geldern and Richard Stites (*Mass Culture in Soviet Russia*) – have examined the difference of opinion between communists like Lenin who believed that the political structure must be changed before a genuine proletarian culture could emerge, and more radical communists who saw the establishment of proletarian culture as a prerequisite of a workers' state. Geldern and Stites highlighted the continuation of existing forms of culture and the difficulty the state encountered in getting the public to consume what it wanted.

Other historians, like Peter Kenez (for example, *The Birth of the Propaganda State: Soviet Methods of Mass Mobilisation 1917–1929*), have emphasised the pervasive nature of communist propaganda immediately after the revolution, and the fact that the Bolsheviks soon succeeded in blocking out alternative points of view to their own. The disillusioned Bolshevik Yevgeny Zamyatin wrote the novel *We* in 1920, satirising the new totalitarianism. It was to influence George Orwell's *1984*, but Zamyatin could not publish the novel in the USSR.

The communists replaced many organisations with their own, particularly the youth movement. They paved the way for the even more intense campaigns of the Stalinist era, which built on earlier attempts and probably had more success in steering a mass audience into the regime's way of thinking.

HOW DIFFERENT WAS LENIN'S RUSSIA FROM TSARIST RUSSIA?

Political structures and practices

Russia was an autocracy under the tsar, and in essence under Lenin also. The tsar had few restrictions on either his legislative or executive powers, although it was accepted that his divine right authority carried with it the responsibility to protect his people. The tsar owned most of the country's resources, and he could demand service from his subjects. His ministers were not responsible to the *duma* once that was established, and the tsar could appoint or remove ministers at will.

Lenin did not have an official government position. However, his position within the Communist Party was unchallenged. Although in theory Russia had a 'dictatorship of the proletariat', in practice decisions were taken by a small group of leading Party members, inside or outside the *Politburo*. Lenin interfered in the smallest detail of government, just like the tsars.

In essence, Russia was a dictatorship before and after the revolution. The differences were that the Communist Party claimed to derive its authority not from God but from the will of the proletariat, and in practice it was more efficient in enforcing its authority. Arguably, Lenin's secret police was more feared than that of the tsar, was more arbitrary in its operations and was responsible for far more deaths and imprisonments.

However, some historians (for example, Pipes) have emphasised the continuity between the repression of pre-revolutionary and post-revolutionary regimes:

> *The tsarist state police developed sophisticated methods of surveillance, infiltrating society through a network of paid informers and opposition parties with the help of professional agents ... Its methods were all too familiar to Russian revolutionaries who, on coming to power, adopted them and turned them against their enemies. The* Cheka *and its successors assimilated the practices of the tsarist state police to such an extent that as late as the 1980s, the KGB distributed to its staff manuals prepared by the* Okhrana *nearly a century earlier* (Pipes, *Russia Under the Bolshevik Regime*).

On the other hand, the Soviet secret police never voluntarily allowed potential opponents to go into exile where they could plot against the regime. Trotsky lived abroad after his fall from power, but was eventually hunted down and killed by a Stalinist agent.

Soviet Russia was the first of the modern one-party dictatorships to use a combination of force and propaganda to maintain a hold on the population. The tsarist regime also used force, censorship and propaganda less efficiently – although additionally it had the advantages of traditional deference and the authority of the Church to reinforce its authority, and for most of its existence it had a wider base of social support.

A major difference was the social composition of the ruling class. The tsarist regime relied on an educated bureaucratic class, as well as the aristocracy. The communist regime used some members of the old bureaucracy, but increasingly created its own bureaucracy of Party members, many of whom came from lower social origins, and had either forged their Party careers during the civil war or had joined the Communist Party in the subsequent years. Both tsarist and communist bureaucracies were free from public scrutiny.

The economy and society

There were important differences as well as similarities between communist and tsarist economy and society. There had been a significant degree of state intervention in the tsarist economy – for example, in railway construction. But there had also been private enterprise, bolstered by investment from abroad. Under the NEP, there was a combination of state control, with the government running the 'commanding heights of the economy' such as the railways and mines. But there was also private enterprise responsible for smaller enterprises and agriculture.

Although the aristocracy lost its land in 1917 and many fled the country between 1917 and 1921, about 100,000 remained in Russia during the 1920s. The middle classes regained some of their influence under the NEP, becoming traders and businessmen. Industrial workers still lived and worked in relatively poor conditions and still had few rights. The unions had little power, and many workers still regarded themselves as being exploited by the government or their employers.

In contrast, many peasants had gained compared with tsarist days. Many of those who had survived the trauma of the civil war and War Communism now had their own land, and the *kulaks*, or richer peasants, did well, although there were divisions between rich and poor peasants. All were relatively free from communist control, since the Communist Party remained weak in the countryside until the period of collectivisation. Very few peasants joined the Communist Party.

In some essentials there were major similarities between Lenin's Russia and tsarist Russia. Both claimed ownership of productive resources; both claimed the right to make citizens work for the state.

Russia in the 1920s was in a state of limbo. The regime had survived the crisis of the civil war, and although facing a hostile capitalist world, had begun to forge relationships with foreign governments based on a desire for trade and foreign expertise. NEP Russia appeared to be recovering, but it was an uneasy period, especially for those in the Communist Party. The NEP was still seen as a compromise, and it was widely accepted that, at some stage, Russia would move to a more socialist form of society, which would involve major dislocations in society as well as the economy. Meanwhile Lenin's successors were manoeuvring for power.

CONCLUSION: HOW SIGNIFICANT WAS LENIN?

Lenin's importance within the USSR was as great in death as in life, and until the break-up of the USSR he was beyond criticism. Even in the 1980s, when the last Soviet leader Gorbachev was trying to implement market reforms in the economy, he invoked Lenin's use of the NEP to give authority to his own reforms. Lenin was at least as important as a symbol as he was a historical figure. His importance can be summarised as follows.

- As an icon, whose name was invoked to justify whatever policies the current Soviet leadership was promoting.
- As a theorist, who adapted Marxism as it suited the needs of the moment or to justify policies like the NEP after the event. It was also Lenin who created the concept of the one-party state and added his own views on subjects such as imperialism, which had not featured prominently in Marx's work. Some commentators like Neil Harding (*Leninism*) have written about Lenin's inconsistencies and unorthodoxy in his beliefs, and have concluded that he was ultimately unimportant as a theorist. However, inconsistent as his theories might be, they gave generations of communists the confidence that whatever they did, it was legitimate.
- As a man of action, without whom it is difficult to imagine the October revolution or the Reds' survival after 1917. Despite his own prominent role in these events, Trotsky conceded Lenin's primacy in his biography of Lenin, published in 1925.

All interpretations of Lenin agree on his importance, even those Soviet historians who followed the orthodox line that individuals were less important than economic and social forces in determining the course of history. Interpretations outside the USSR varied. Sympathisers regarded Lenin as an inspiration both to Russia and exploited classes everywhere. Those opposing this view regarded him as a ruthless power-driven dictator, a precursor of Stalin and a leader responsible for enormous suffering. Most interpretations were between these two extremes.

More sympathetic views have tended to emphasise Lenin's idealism and genuine concern for ordinary people. The excesses of the post-revolutionary period are explained by the chaotic condition of Russia in the civil war, which encouraged excesses on both sides. Sympathisers also point to Lenin's willingness to adapt policies in 1921, and the fact that Lenin himself agonised in his last years about the growth of the bureaucracy, something he never foresaw.

More critical interpretations suggest that Lenin himself was responsible for the situation he bemoaned, that he was personally responsible for the terror. Had he lived longer, there would have been further dislocations in Russia, although perhaps his excesses would not have been on the scale of Stalin's. What all historians agree on is that Lenin had a profound influence on the Russian revolution and subsequent period, for good or ill.

Only as recently as the late-1980s onwards have Russian historians begun to criticise aspects of Lenin's rule – for example, his treatment of opponents. Those like Dmitri Volkogonov, a former Red Army officer who had access to previously unreleased files, have been critical of Lenin's authoritarianism, which prevented Russia taking the path of democratic development:

> To flourish, communism needed a military threat, and both domestic and foreign enemies. The defeat of Leninism was programmed by history. Lenin had only one chance to save it: he could have preserved political pluralism after October 1917 and given scope to social democratic aspirations and traditions. But that would not have been the Leninist way (Volkogonov, *Lenin: A New Biography*).

Western interpretations of Lenin were always more varied. Some Marxist sympathisers like Christopher Hill (in *Lenin and the Russian Revolution*) have praised Lenin as leader of the oppressed. The so-called 'liberal' historians were critical of Lenin since they were hostile to the authoritarian communist regime and its policies, and apportioned a major share of the responsibility for these to Lenin. Exponents of this view include Leonard Schapiro and, in more recent years, Richard Pipes. Pipes in particular has been extremely critical:

> Lenin owes his historical prominence not to his statesmanship, which was of a very inferior order, but to his generalship. He was one of history's great conquerors ... he was the first head of state to treat politics, domestic as well as foreign, as warfare in the literal sense of the word, the objective of which was not to compel the enemy to submit but to annihilate him ... It did not help him build a viable social and political order ... Judged in terms of its own aspirations, the communist regime was a monumental

failure: it succeeded in one thing only, staying in power. But since for Bolsheviks power was not an end in itself but means to an end, its mere retention does not qualify the experiment as a success (Pipes, *Russia Under the Bolshevik Regime*).

In his collection of previously unpublished sources (*The Unknown Lenin*), Pipes presented Lenin as a manipulative, ruthless dictator with 'utter disregard for human life' and scorn for individual human beings, with particular contempt for Russians: 'In dealing with non-Bolsheviks, he either played on fear or appealed to greed. To dominate the human beings under his control, he resorted to unbridled violence.'

Revisionist historians such as Sheila Fitzpatrick (*The Russian Revolution 1917–1932*) and Robert Service (*Lenin: A Political Life*) have tended to downplay Lenin's importance – for example, by focusing on the difficulties he sometimes encountered in imposing his will on colleagues. Historians now frequently analyse less overtly political trends – for example, studying what happened at grass-roots level in the factories and on the farms, believing that there is too much emphasis on politicians.

The debate about Lenin's significance will continue, because it is bound up with the Russian revolution, itself one of the most significant events of the twentieth century. The works of historians like Service, Edward Acton (*Rethinking the Russian Revolution*) and Geoffrey Hosking (*A History of the Soviet Union*) are quite balanced, but interpretations will continue to change as the events of this period, as of any important historical era, are seen from a new perspective.

PART 2

Stalinist Russia, 1924–53

KEY QUESTIONS

- How did Stalin become leader of the USSR by 1929?
- How successful was the New Economic Policy? (NEP)
- Why did the USSR implement policies of rapid collectivisation and industrialisation?
- What impact did collectivisation and the Five Year Plans have on the Soviet economy and society?
- What were the motives for the Great Terror?
- What impact did the Great Terror have on the USSR?
- How fundamentally was the USSR changed by the Stalin revolution of 1928–41?
- To what extent was the USSR a totalitarian state by 1941?
- What impact did the war of 1941–5 have on the USSR?
- To what extent had the USSR recovered from the effects of war by 1953?
- What similarities and differences were there between Stalin's Russia and the Russia of his predecessors?

THE LEADERSHIP STRUGGLE

The struggle for the succession to Lenin was already going on before his death in 1924, partly because he was seriously ill and partly because he did gave no clear indications about what should happen after his death. Lenin's famous **Testament** was not particularly enthusiastic about any of the leading communists, and its postscript was positively damning in its assessment of Stalin's qualities. It seemed to be advocating some kind of collective leadership.

Of the leading contenders, Trotsky may have seemed the obvious choice, given his prominence during the revolutionary and civil war period. But Trotsky was suspect to many communists because of his Menshevik background, his arrogance and fears about his intentions. He felt that being Jewish would work against him (that is, he thought that anti-Semitic prejudice might be a problem for the Party if he was chosen as leader). Trotsky also lacked a power base within the Communist Party.

KEY TERM

Lenin's Testament
Written in the months before his death in 1924, in this document Lenin considered the qualities of his colleagues such as Trotsky, Stalin, Zinoviev, Kamenev and Bukharin. He found fault with all of them as possible successors, and presumably wanted some sort of collective leadership to succeed him, although he was very definite in insisting that Stalin was unsuitable to follow him as leader. The controversial nature of the Testament meant that it was suppressed for a time after Lenin's death for fear of causing factional arguments in the Communist Party.

Kamenev and Zinoviev were leading communists, but had made 'mistakes' in the past such as opposing the decision to mount a *coup* in October 1917. Additionally, they were prone to factionalism.

Stalin was building up a strong power base in the Communist Party through his role as General Secretary. However, he was not regarded by his colleagues as a serious contender, and was generally felt to lack the intellect and personality to become leader.

NEP RUSSIA

Although there is sometimes a tendency to focus on the personality clashes and changing alliances during the 1920s as leading communists manoeuvred and argued for influence, theoretical arguments were also very important during this period.

All communists believed in industrialisation as the precondition of socialism. While still committed to the idea of spreading revolution around the world, there was a growing acceptance that, at least for the time being, Russia would have to go it alone. Stalin's espousal of 'socialism in one country' appeared to be more in tune with Russia's needs than Trotsky's 'permanent revolution'.

Many communists were uneasy about the NEP. While it appeared to be reaping economic benefits, particularly for groups such as the *kulaks*, it did not represent socialism, nor could it promise a secure economic future. The **'Scissors crisis'** of 1923 showed the problems caused by disparities between agricultural and industrial prices. The reluctance of peasants in the later 1920s to release cheap grain on to the market prompted the regime into requisitioning reminiscent of the civil war period, and eventually led to collectivisation. Arguments about how industrialisation could be paid for dominated many Party debates.

STALIN'S TRIUMPH

Factionalism had not been destroyed by the unity edict of 1921. The alliance made before Lenin's death by Zinoviev, Kamenev and Stalin to keep out Trotsky did not survive personal bickering and policy disagreements. After Lenin's death, Stalin kept his power base because the leadership was reluctant to publish and act on Lenin's Testament and reveal differences among the leadership.

The mid-1920s saw shifting alliances as Zinoviev and Kamenev formed an alliance with Trotsky, until all three fell from grace and lost power and influence. One of the major historiographical debates centred on the responsibility for Stalin's rise to power. Was it primarily due to the mistakes of his opponents? Or was it due to his own skill?

How ambitious was Stalin? It is clear that, even when he did not directly create situations that directly benefited himself, he knew how to take advantage of those opportunities that did arise. Having outmanoeuvred those on the left with the aid of the right, he turned on the latter, forcing leading figures such as Bukharin out of the limelight and effectively securing the leadership by 1929.

ECONOMIC AND SOCIAL REVOLUTION

The great economic and social revolution that transformed Russia into a leading world power began with forced collectivisation and industrialisation in 1928. There has been considerable debate about the impact of collectivisation. Was the fact that the countryside had been brought under communist control and food supplies secured proof of success, despite the enormous human cost involved in eliminating *kulaks* and the horrific results of famine? Or was the fact that agriculture remained inefficient proof of its failure? Was collectivisation a prerequisite for the success of the industrialisation programme?

The Five Year Plans have also produced considerable controversy. They clearly had a massive impact on production figures in heavy industry, but there is dispute about the exact extent. The plans were a great experiment. But how coherent was the overall strategy? How effective was it in practice? Were the plans responsible for giving the USSR the industrial and military base that enabled it to withstand the German assault of 1941 and emerge from the war as a leading world power? In social terms, what impact did industrialisation have on Soviet society?

TERROR

The 1930s are also very much associated with the Great Terror, launched after the assassination of Sergei Kirov in 1934. It was generally accepted that whatever role Stalin may have played in the assassination, he used the event to his advantage to purge real or imagined opponents of the regime. The Great Terror that ensued resulted in the execution or imprisonment of millions of Russians, both Party members and others. Leading old Bolsheviks were given show trials before they disappeared.

The debate among historians concerns Stalin's motives. Was this a cynical ploy to find scapegoats for failures, to prevent opposition and create a siege mentality that would make the population accept any sacrifices? Or was he simply mentally unbalanced or bent on revenge?

But there have also been debates about how far Stalin was actually in control of the whole process, and to what extent the purges operated under their own momentum. Linked with this debate is the issue of the extent to which the USSR was a monolithic, totalitarian state. The regime controlled every aspect of people's lives. But to what extent did ordinary Russians believe what they were told? How effective was the propaganda? Or did the regime rely on terror?

WAR AND VICTORY

One unforeseen result of the purges, whether they were planned or otherwise, was the devastating effect they had on the leadership of the Red Army, which was inadequately prepared to face the German attack of June 1941. Stalin appears to have been caught unawares, although there is plenty of evidence to suggest that he must have had some inkling of what was in store, despite signing the Nazi–Soviet Non-Aggression Pact with Hitler in 1939.

The war was devastating for the USSR in terms of material damage and human cost, and the USSR survived the initial German attacks with great difficulty. Most historians accept that it was the Soviet contribution on the Eastern Front that was primarily responsible for fatally weakening the German war effort. More open to debate are the quality of Stalin's leadership and the reasons for the ultimate Soviet victory.

Historians have often focused on the German 'mistakes' during the campaign and the heroism of the Red Army soldier in bringing about the eventual Soviet victory. However, there is considerable evidence to suggest that the unified leadership under Stalin and the pre-war effort to industrialise Russia were also crucial factors, and made the Soviet victory almost inevitable once the German campaign ran out of steam.

STALINISM

What is indisputable is that the USSR emerged from the war materially weakened but morally and psychologically triumphant, with Stalin now not just leader of his country but also a statesman on the world stage, controlling the destiny of a large chunk of eastern and central Europe. Many of the features of the pre-war Russia were present after 1945, including renewed purges and a massive programme to restore the economy.

Stalin's position was unchallengeable. At the time of his death, 'Stalinism' was equated with Russian nationalism and a particular form of political, social and economic organisation: a command economy in which the regime established the priorities, and an authoritarian rule reinforced by propaganda and the threat of force, all under the direction of a Party that tried to control all organisations and means of expression.

Was this totalitarianism? Was Stalinism fundamentally different from Leninism? Indeed, is this a useful concept for analysing what had happened in the USSR?

1 How did Stalin become leader of the USSR by 1929?

BACKGROUND

Historians have never been able to agree on exactly how Stalin became undisputed leader of the USSR and established a personal dictatorship, although the dating of his rise can now be established with some confidence.

The *Politburo* was meeting weekly in the 1920s, but it met far less often from 1929 and there was less discussion of policy. By 1933, the Secretariat was no longer meeting, and the *Orgburo* met less often. Documents were sent to these bodies for signing, but not for discussing. From 1929, Stalin increasingly dealt with individuals on a face-to-face basis in his office and decisions were individual rather than collective.

STALIN'S QUALITIES

Stalin's rise to this position was facilitated by a combination of luck, skill on his part, and the mistakes and miscalculations of his rivals. There has often been a reluctance to acknowledge Stalin's skill in the manoeuvrings of the 1920s. This is partly due to the verdict of his contemporaries, who were all too ready to dismiss him as a 'grey blur'. Stalin lacked the charisma of a Trotsky, but he did have other advantages.

- He already had the reputation of being a good administrator and had originally been promoted because he was good at getting things done. This had been a trait from his early days, when he had stayed in Russia working among the grass roots of the Bolshevik Party while many of its leaders, including Lenin, were in exile abroad.
- His determination, or obstinacy, was also evident in the civil war, when he first fell out with Trotsky. Stalin's skills were acknowledged by Lenin, who appointed him to the *Politburo*, the *Orgburo* and the Secretariat, as well as making him General Secretary of the Communist Party. This latter position in particular gave Stalin a good power base. Particularly after **the Lenin Enrolment** had brought many more workers into the Communist Party, dependent on Stalin's goodwill for advancement, he could count on support in the Communist Party debates.
- Stalin was adept at turning situations to his particular advantage. This occurred notably after Lenin's death when Stalin took advantage of the funeral arrangements and assumed the mantle of Lenin's authority to

KEY TERM

The Lenin Enrolment
Launched after Lenin's death early in 1924, this was the first major recruitment drive to the Communist Party, and brought in over 200,000 recruits. Many were young, working-class recruits, who provided support for Stalin in his forthcoming battles with the more experienced Bolshevik Old Guard.

justify his own policies and discredit those of rivals. He also took advantage of other's errors – for example, Trotsky's attack on the bureaucracy, which smacked of opportunism and factionalism.

- Far from being a 'grey blur', Stalin showed considerable skill in the debates of the 1920s in presenting himself as the 'unity' candidate, a man of the centre, letting others make their move first, then altering his own position as seemed advantageous.

Opportunist, or man of principle?

Some interpretations of Stalin have overplayed his 'luck' or 'peasant cunning' and implied that his career was consumed by unbridled ambition from the start. This is a dubious interpretation.

For years before the revolution, Stalin, the outsider from Georgia, had been one of those Bolsheviks known for 'getting things done' – for example, robbing banks to raise money for Party funds while more intellectual Bolsheviks theorised. For an ambitious politician, joining the Bolsheviks in tsarist Russia would not have seemed a good career move.

However, no historian has ever satisfactorily explained either the stage in the 1920s when Stalin decided to make a move for power or the extent to which he really believed in the various causes he espoused.

Did Stalin really believe in 'socialism in one country', or was it just a tactic to help portray Trotsky as an irresponsible adventurer in his calls for permanent revolution, which threatened to embroil Russia in risky foreign adventures? When Stalin decided in 1926 that the NEP was no longer tenable, was this a genuine policy conversion or a tactic to defeat the right? After all, up to this point he had been regarded as a moderate in economic policy.

Stalin's opponents naturally accused him of opportunism. They claimed he was adopting the policies of the left after defeating its main representatives such as Trotsky. But other communists had also changed their ideological stance. For example, Bukharin, who had been opposed to the NEP, became one of its principal supporters. Yet he was rarely accused of opportunism.

All interpretations of Stalin's rise to power face the problem that genuine arguments over economic policy were intertwined with personal battles for influence and power, and it is therefore difficult to distinguish between principle and opportunism. Also, because of Stalin's later reputation for ruthlessness and even paranoia in the 1930s, there is a danger of letting this knowledge colour views of his actions in the 1920s.

It may be that Stalin genuinely accepted the NEP in its early years because it appeared to be working, but later changed his view when it became clear that it could not solve Russia's long-term problems of industrial backwardness. Did this represent pragmatism rather than cynicism? Were practical considerations as important as personal ambition in determining Stalin's actions in the 1920s?

INTERPRETATIONS

Many western historians have emphasised the personal qualities of Stalin in analysing his rise to power, describing his manipulative qualities and personal drive for power. Typical of this approach are Robert Tucker (*Stalin As Revolutionary 1879–1929: a Study in History and Personality*) and Robert Conquest (*Stalin: The Breaker of Nations*).

Although not sympathetic to Stalin, some historians were more inclined to play down the element of personal ambition and focus more on the political structures that allowed an individual to emerge as leader. Typical of this approach is Edward Carr in *The Bolshevik Revolution 1917–1923*. Sometimes labelled 'structuralists' because of their detailed analysis of the structure of the Communist Party and the Russian state, these historians tend to emphasise the importance of Stalin's role as General Secretary in giving him the opportunity to build up influence through the Communist Party organisation.

Because they have focused on structures rather than personalities, historians like Robert Service (*The Bolshevik Party in Revolution: a Study in Organisational Change 1917–23*) have emphasised the continuity of experience between the Leninist and post-Leninist periods. These views are echoed to a large extent in post-Soviet historiography of Stalin – for example, by Dmitri Volkogonov in *Stalin: Triumph and Tragedy*. While Volkogonov conceded that Stalin showed considerable tactical skill at key points, he painted an unflattering portrait of his intellectual make-up:

> *Stalin was a strong personality of the type that strives only for greatness and unlimited power … For Stalin the moral parameters of the revolution and the building of a new world were nothing more than bourgeois moralising. Nor did he have the least doubts about his own moral rightness. In a book by the nineteenth-century Russian anarchist Bakunin, he underlined the phrase: 'Don't waste time on doubting yourself, because that is the biggest waste of time ever invented by man'* (Volkogonov, *Stalin: Triumph and Tragedy*).

Later Russian historians were prepared to argue that Stalin was essentially a product of Leninism, which had paved the way for an ambitious individual to take advantage of the authoritarian Party structure created after the revolution. This represents a distinct change from Soviet interpretations of Stalin.

While Stalin was alive, 'official' biographical studies of him such as G. Alexandrov's *Joseph Stalin: A Short Biography* (1947) were little more than idolatry. In contrast, Trotsky's interpretation of Stalin was inevitably coloured by his need to explain his defeat by a rival whom he regarded as far inferior in intellect and ability. Trotsky's argument in books such as his own work *The Revolution Betrayed* was that the Russian revolution spawned not a workers' state but a giant, corrupt bureaucracy which allowed Stalin, the arch-bureaucrat, to worm his way to the top.

From 1956 onwards there was criticism of Stalin, but it was couched in a way that emphasised his differences from Lenin, and there was no criticism of the Communist Party itself. In other words, there was no suggestion that the political structure was faulty in allowing an individual like Stalin to make his way to the top.

The local picture

The main developments in historiography since the 1980s have been to examine 1920s Russia from a wider perspective – in other words, focusing less on the personalities of Stalin and his opponents, and examining a much broader range of factors such as social and economic developments, the development of the Communist Party structure and the role of ideology.

Merle Fainsod had already done this in 1958 by examining archives from the city of Smolensk (*Smolensk Under Soviet Rule*). He demonstrated that, until 1927, life in the city had scarcely been affected by the political controversies in Moscow. It was difficult to implement change in an area with its own strong traditions and surrounded by a largely peasant population. Only when the regime began to implement collectivisation and industrialisation did things begin to change, and Party members began to identify with the dictates from Moscow rather than with their own local concerns.

Stalin's take-over of power: Moscow

Very few historians have given a convincing picture of what Stalin's take-over of power looked like on the ground, by looking at developments in a particular place. A study of Moscow gives a clearer idea of how Stalin won. Moscow was one of the few significant centres in Russia whose Party organisation was still controlled by the right until October 1928, under the local Party secretary N.A. Uglanov. He was defeated by a mixture of blackmail and threats. He also suffered from unpopularity resulting from economic recession in the late 1920s, which led to a 25 per cent unemployment rate among adult males.

Stalin's support came from hard-line Party militants in their late 20s and 30s, who had often cut their teeth in the civil war. While not inherently hostile to groups like the peasantry, they were prepared to go into action if they were persuaded that force was necessary. They had not been prepared to support Trotsky when he had advocated tough measures, because he was seen as a factionalist.

Trotsky's supporters had been removed from Moscow by 1928. Karl Bauman, First Secretary of the Moscow Party organisation from 1929, outdid Stalin in his hard line approach. It was Bauman who first used the phrase 'liquidation of the *kulaks* as a class'. Under Bauman, Party officials, anxious to prove their loyalty and remove any suspicion of rightist tendencies – an important consideration since show trials had already begun in 1928 – pursued the new policy of collectivisation with unrestrained zeal. Their zeal was so great that the Central Committee dismissed Bauman and over 100 officials in Moscow, because peasant unrest was causing disquiet. Bauman's successor was Lazar Kaganovich, a Stalin loyalist. Further discipline was imposed on the Moscow Party with a halt to recruitment and with police officials attending Party meetings.

The importance of these events is that they show the importance of dynamic action coming from below, sometimes moving ahead of the Communist Party, and show that events were not always driven by the leadership. Stalin's skill was in locking into the dynamism of the rank and file activists and also that of the more established Party elite, and indeed fusing the two.

CONCLUSION

The example of Moscow demonstrates how historians should look beyond the debates and intrigue that went on inside the Kremlin during this period. It is also important to look at Stalin's career in the 1920s from a broader perspective, as Chris Ward has done. He emphasised that:

> The difficulties of governing inflated the importance of administration, a factor never envisaged by Bolshevism's founder until the moment of his death. Governing required consensus in and between society and state, but this was in short supply. Ruling required strong and stable channels for the exercise of power, but these had been smashed by revolution and war. Consequently, the enigmas of governing and ruling resolved themselves into problems of administration, and these in turn became matters of establishing and servicing a bureaucratic machine. The Soviet regime's power structures thus emerged independently of its constitutional structures – weakly formulated in any case – and Stalin stood at the focal point of this development. Given Lenin's death (which threw the leadership into

disarray), a modicum of popular support (evident among the metropolitan proletariat in 1928) and his mastery of the apparatus (staffed by the new cohort of sub-elites thrown up after 1917), circumstances ensured that inside the mutating body of the party-state he would succeed and his rivals fail (Ward, *Stalin's Russia*).

It is important to remember that whatever the trends in 1920s Russia, Stalin still had to display personal skills in order to take advantage of these trends and emerge as undisputed leader.

2 How fundamentally was the USSR changed by the Stalinist revolution of 1928–41?

THE BACKGROUND: NEP RUSSIA

Historians have sometimes focused more on the manoeuvrings for power in the mid- and late-1920s than the social and economic backdrop to Party intrigues. However, some historians like Sheila Fitzpatrick, Alexander Rabinowitch and Richard Stites (*Russia in the Era of NEP: Explorations in Soviet Society and Culture*), and Vladimir Brovkin (*Russia After Lenin*), have emphasised that NEP Russia was, socially and economically, a society in transition. Brovkin called it 'an independent and vibrant society'.

The communists had eliminated organised opposition but did not yet feel secure in 1920s Russia, which was a diverse society despite the communists' monopoly of power reinforced through their use of agitation, propaganda and invocation of class warfare.

Historians like Peter Kenez (for example, *The Birth of the Propaganda State*) have analysed the various ways by which the communists used propaganda and education to create their own 'world view' of society. Their message was clearly successful in influencing Party activists. But other historians doubted their success in convincing the population as a whole. Was there a clash between the regime's agenda of building a modern socialist society and the immediate localised concerns of ordinary Russians?

Popular attitudes

There has been increasing evidence that many sections of society found communist attitudes irritating or patronising, and that communist attempts to promote a new communist mentality and values had a limited impact.

Peasants were particularly resistant to change. Although content with the economic arrangements of NEP, they did not welcome any other interference in their lives. However, many workers also disliked communist attitudes and felt that they worked in conditions similar to those of the old tsarist regime. They were generally apathetic towards politics.

While some historians have assumed that the impact of communist propaganda on the young was considerable, others, like Brovkin, claim that the *Komsomol* – the communist youth movement – was more interested in creating mischief against institutions like the Church, without any serious interest in 'building socialism.' There is evidence of working class youth defying the new communist morality, being more interested in vodka than Marx.

Women still suffered discrimination in the workplace and at home, despite notional equality. There were complaints that already the Communist Party had degenerated into a self-serving bureaucracy more interested in preserving its privileges than promoting socialism. The Party archives show that Stalin and other members of the *Politburo* knew the difficulties they faced and were well aware that the Communist Party had not succeeded in implanting an attitude of class consciousness in the population at large. They knew this because they had regular reports on popular attitudes culled from police reports. These reports were not couched in the usual propaganda, but rather were frank in their appraisal of popular moods.

Brovkin went so far as to affirm that Stalin and the central apparatus of the Communist Party instituted the 'second revolution' not just because of a concern about food supplies from the countryside following the requisitioning crisis of 1927. It was also a pre-emptive strike against the peasantry and even against complacent members of the Communist Party, because there was a fear that the communists had not succeeded in firmly establishing themselves in power up until this point.

Therefore, the economic revolution from 1928 onwards was not just about building a socialist economic system and making Russia a great power, but about strengthening the control of the central Party apparatus over the provinces and even Party cliques at the local level. It was a cultural and social revolution as well as a political one.

ECONOMIC AND SOCIAL REVOLUTION

Stalin's drive to collectivise and industrialise marked the start of a key era in Soviet history, because it established the norms of Soviet life for the rest of the USSR's existence. There was continuity with pre-1917 Russia in so far as the tsarist state had been heavily involved in industrial development. However, Russia had then been a predominantly market economy, and also a rural one, in which agricultural production had risen at a greater rate proportionately than the population – unlike 1920s Russia. The 1930s shifted the emphasis towards industrial production, and in the 1930s capital goods production grew at a considerably greater rate than before 1914.

Stalin had evident economic motives. Apart from the desire to 'create socialism', it was clear that, although there had been a considerable economic recovery in some respects under the NEP (particularly in the volume of foreign trade), the economy had not regained pre-war levels. Hence the emphasis after 1928 on massive increases in output.

At socio economic imperative

How effective were Soviet methods? Although many historians have been dismissive of Soviet statistics, the Russians were pioneers in statistical analysis, and the figures for the 1920s are probably as reliable as those from most countries. This was no longer true in the 1930s, because economic statistics in the USSR were either distorted or simply not published in the first place. Therefore, there has inevitably been a debate about the effectiveness of the three Five Year Plans in existence between 1928 and 1941.

Most historians have agreed that, whatever the precise figures, there was a considerable increase in the output of most capital goods, providing the basis for further economic development. In contrast, consumer goods were given a relatively low priority. There was a major decline in agricultural output, as farming struggled to recover from the trauma of collectivisation.

There are several main conclusions to be drawn about economic development in the 1930s. The regime was successful in directing a high proportion of gross national product into investment and ensuring that priority sectors such as defence got the benefits of what advanced technology was available. However, the regime was far less successful in developing agricultural production, although it did secure food supplies for the towns. Consumers suffered from shortages ranging from housing to everyday items, although once the dust had settled on the peasant war and famine of the early 1930s, the basics of food supplies were assured. Production figures in some industrial sectors were impressive in terms of quality, but masked the fact that technological innovation was not encouraged in most sectors, and the system was inefficiently managed.

Overall, the judgement of many historians is that the drive to industrialise was successful in so far as the USSR secured an industrial base that helped it to win the 1941–5 war and become an industrial power. In the long run it was not successful, because the crude top-down model of the command economy was inflexible, inefficient and discouraged initiative in the drive to meet crude quantitative targets rather than concern itself with quality.

For a backward country like the USSR, the initial gains were impressive. But the model was not suited to the needs of a more sophisticated economy once the groundwork had been done. This problem was to bedevil Stalin's successors. However, they never resolved it because the Stalinist system they inherited was resistant to change.

The fundamental rationale of the economic revolution is still open to debate. Historians like Edward Carr believed that the NEP was fundamentally unstable and that the demands of modern economics made some form of state planning necessary. This view is shared by some post-Soviet Russian historians. A few western historians, like Robert Tucker (*Stalin As Revolutionary 1879–1929: A Study in History and Personality*), support the Bukharin view that the NEP could have been compatible with longer-term economic development without the dislocation caused by Stalin's methods.

Many economic historians like R.W. Davis, Mark Harrison and S.G. Wheatcroft (*The Economic Transformation of the Soviet Union 1913–1945*) have adopted a balanced view that a moderate expansion of industry and agriculture was a viable proposition in late 1920s Russia, but that it would not have been possible to achieve a higher rate of industrialisation than had occurred before 1914 without a major transformation, which depended on the political ambitions of Stalin.

A 1929 poster satirising the enemies of progress represented by the Five Year Plan. They include the drunkard, the priest, the plutocrat, the lying journalist and the Menshevik.

ВРАГИ ПЯТИЛЕТКИ

ПОМЕЩИК СМОТРИТ ЗЛЫМ БАРБОСОМ, КУЛАК СОПИТ БУГРИСТЫМ НОСОМ, ПЬЯНЧУГА С ГОРЯ ПЬЕТ ЗАПОЕМ, ПОП ОГОЛТЕЛЫМ ВОЕТ ВОЕМ,

ШИПИТ ПРОДАЖНЫЙ ЖУРНАЛИСТ, ОСТРИТ КЛЫКИ КАПИТАЛИСТ, МЕНЬШЕВИЧОК ВО-ВСЮ ЯРИТЯ, ВОЯКА БЕЛЫЙ МАТЕРИТСЯ,—

ПСЫ, НЕ ПОСАЖЕННЫЕ В КЛЕТКУ, ВСЕ, КТО СТОИТ ЗА СТАРИНУ, ЗЛО ПРОКЛИНАЮТ ПЯТИЛЕТКУ И ОБЪЯВЛЯЮТ ЕЙ ВОЙНУ,

ГРОЗЯТ ЕЙ СРЫВОМ, ПОНИМАЯ, ЧТО В НЕЙ — ПОГИБЕЛЬ ИХ ПРЯМАЯ!

ДЕМЬЯН БЕДНЫЙ

THE PHASES OF DEVELOPMENT

One of the difficulties in interpreting the period of the Five Year Plans has been a tendency to see the period from 1928 to 1941 as a whole, when in reality there were several distinct phases, as identified by Davis, Harrison and Wheatcroft.

1928–30. This was a period of accelerating industrialisation, urbanisation and forcible collectivisation. Shortages led to rationing in the towns, but at the same time the regime was promising a Utopian future.

1930–2. During these years, economic policy was confused, reflecting the fact that the initial 'plans' had never been properly planned at all. Attempts to fulfil the targets of over-ambitious plans approved in July 1930 actually led to a decline in the rate of industrial growth. There was a slight relaxation of the regime's draconian approach. The free peasant market was legalised and quotas on deliveries from collective farms were reduced.

1933. Despite the disastrous 1932 harvest (there is an argument that Stalin deliberately allowed this crisis to become worse than it need have been), grain quotas were increased. Other policies and targets were more realistic – including those in the more modest second Five Year Plan.

1934–6. This was a period of spectacular economic development, as factories built during the first plan began to produce and agriculture slowly recovered. The standard of living rose and rationing was abolished. These improvements took place against a backdrop of increased repression.

1937–41. These years were a period of mass repression and also preparations for war. The disruption of the purges caused a slowing down of industrial production, despite a tightening up of labour discipline.

THE DEBATE OVER METHODS AND SUCCESS

The methods
At one level, western historians have been very critical of Stalin's methods – particularly since the economic changes were inextricably bound up with the regime's use of terror as a political and economic weapon.

It was difficult to justify the forcible collectivisation of agriculture, or specifically the treatment of *kulaks* (a term extended to any peasant labelled as an enemy of the state), who were killed, deported or forced to seek work on industrial projects. Some areas, notably Ukraine, were

A 1933 Soviet poster proclaiming the triumphs of the first Five Year Plan. In 1928, the bourgeois opponent of communism laughs at the ambitions of the Plan. Five years later he is stunned and angered by the achievements of industrialisation.

devastated by famine. The population as a whole was exhorted to make sacrifices for a better future and there was no mercy for slackers or doubters.

Economic historians have tried to put these changes into context, pointing out that brutal change from above was part of a long tradition in Russia. What was new was the scale and ferocity of Stalin's methods.

Alec Nove also concluded that once a decision to change had been made, it was difficult to 'make omelettes without breaking eggs' (*An Economic History of the USSR*).

Robert Conquest was one of those western historians who condemned Stalin's methods as not only brutal but also unnecessary. Dekulakisation and famine did not have to go hand in hand with collectivisation. In his view, the famine in Ukraine was deliberately engineered by Stalin (*The Harvest of Sorrow*).

Some historians have emphasised that it is impossible to divorce the economic changes from the ideology. Hiroaki Kuromiya (*Stalin's Industrial Revolution: Politics and Workers 1928–1932*) claimed that too many historians underestimate the importance of the ideology of class warfare that was promoted as part of the Five Year Plans, even though the regime found it had to incorporate many despised capitalist mechanisms into the industrial process – allowing increased differentiation of wages between different workers, incorporating capitalist notions of money and trade, and offering incentives to 'bourgeois specialists'.

The link between industrialisation and collectivisation has also created debate among historians. Most believe that the two were inextricably linked partly because food had to be provided for industrial workers and this could be better secured when collective farms had their prime duty to supply quotas of food to the state, and partly because peasants could provide industrial labour. This is why historians like Nove believe that the peasants were the major losers in the process.

Some historians believe that the bulk of the workforce suffered, not just peasants. For example, Peter Kenez wrote:

> *The answer to the question of who paid for Soviet industrialisation is simple. Primarily the peasants paid. Hundreds of thousands of them lost their property through confiscation and were forced to work as convict labourers. Those who stayed in their villages had not only their way of life and institutions taken away, but also most of their food. Much of the peasantry was condemned to starvation. But the workers also paid: their standard of living declined, and they lived in misery* (Kenez, *A History of the Soviet Union From the Beginning to the End*).

However, some historians have seen such interpretations as too simplistic. James Millar (*The Soviet Rural Community*) and others argued that the balance was not so heavily weighted against the peasants, and that deliveries to the towns were smaller than is often believed, while many peasants were still able to buy consumer goods from the towns.

The success
Measuring the success depends on the criteria used. Success for whom?

In the short term. Stalin achieved his objective of eliminating the peasantry as a potentially independent force, resistant to socialist ideology. Once the battle for collectivisation was over, the countryside was quiescent, and Stalin had secured a regular supply of food to the growing towns and industrial workforce. There was rapid industrialisation in the towns. There were massive increases in fuel production and in the engineering industry. Existing industrial centres such as Leningrad and Moscow were further expanded, while new centres of industry were built in outlying republics. Stalin succeeded through propaganda and terror in convincing the population that it must work hard for the future of Russia. He inculcated a siege mentality and reinforced his own position as undisputed leader. Whether the working population regarded the Five Year Plans as successful is more open to question. Unemployment disappeared, but working conditions were difficult. The workforce did not become more efficient. Most of the increased production was due to new workers – sometimes ex-peasants, but frequently women – joining the workforce. Many workers simply worked harder, and successes were built on man and woman power rather than mechanical power.

In the medium term. There was success here. Soviet industry made a great leap forward in the sheer quantities of production achieved. Agriculture

A cartoon in the Soviet magazine *Krokodil*, 1939, showing the peasant's 'selfish' pride in his private plot while the collective fields are neglected. The theme of this cartoon was constantly repeated until the 1980s.

recovered somewhat, particularly when peasants were given concessions such as the right to trade their surplus produce. The army was modernised. The industrialisation programme, and particularly the strategic placing of some industries far in the east, was a crucial factor in Russia's success in war against Germany.

In the long run. The economic revolution was probably a long-term failure, and definitely so if the human cost is taken into account. Agriculture remained a problem. It was characterised by low yields and a peasantry more keen to work on its small private plots than on the collectives. Periodically, grains had to be purchased from abroad. The system of planning in industry prevented the Soviet economy from modernising, and attempts to catch up with the USA, let alone overtake it, ultimately ruined the Soviet economy. The economy was labour intensive. It could not produce the consumer goods that people wanted. Eventually economic problems undermined the entire Soviet regime.

CONCLUSION

There is unlikely ever to be complete agreement on the impact of Stalin's economic revolution, partly because of different definitions of success and failure and the varied perspectives of those involved. A dispossessed *kulak*, for example, would feel very differently about the measures than a skilled engineer who benefited from the higher wages paid to specialists.

What is clear, however, is that Stalin had not built socialism, despite the massive steps taken by the state and Party to control the economy. Collective farmers could still trade freely on the market after the state quota had been met. Specialists could earn more. Consumers could spend their money as they liked, if there were goods and services available. In some industries, employees were still free to change jobs.

Therefore, the economy still had many market features, and socialism had to be redefined as a money, rather than a money-less, economy. It was not a socialism that Marx would have recognised, although the structure of the economy had changed largely beyond recognition in comparison with tsarist days.

3 Why did a totalitarian regime develop in the USSR by 1941?

STALINISM

Historians sometimes debate whether the concept of totalitarianism is a useful term to apply to a regime such as Stalin's USSR. However, most agree that in the 1930s Russia exhibited many of the features normally associated with the term.

The regime tried every method at its disposal to control not only people's everyday lives but also even their thought processes by monopolising all sources of information. Some historians have defined what they regard as the essence of 'Stalinism', although the phrase was never employed in Stalin's USSR. One such definition comes from Graeme Gill (*Stalinism*). He defined the main elements of Stalinism as:

- a highly centralised economic system or 'command economy', with the priority being given to the expansion of heavy industry
- a social structure that initially allowed considerable mobility with people rising through the Communist Party ranks, but that then hardened into a conservative hierarchy of privileges in which those in the senior ranks preserved those privileges and became increasingly resistant to change
- a cultural system that subordinated all cultural and intellectual life to the political demands of the regime
- personal dictatorship reinforced by coercion
- the total politicisation of life, in which no one could 'opt out' of the prevailing political and social consensus
- a dominant conservative ethos, which replaced the initial revolutionary one.

These characteristics were typical of the USSR for most of its existence. However, the emphasis sometimes changed. In the 1930s there was not such a secure hierarchy of privilege, since no one could feel safe from denunciation and removal in the Terror. But by the time of Brezhnev it was certainly the case that those in power generally stayed there, as the increasing ages of those at the top testified, and the USSR became a very conservative society. In contrast, the more overt elements of repression, particularly as represented by the secret police, became toned down, although the threat of state coercion was always in the background.

The reality of political control in the 1930s was very different from the theory. The dictatorship of the proletariat really meant the dictatorship of Stalin. No political institution could challenge Stalin's policies. Organisations like the *Politburo* met less and less frequently. The 1936 constitution promised civil rights, but the Communist Party had no rival centres of power, and citizens had no redress against the abuse of state or Party power.

Stalin relied on the loyalty of Party zealots, many of whom had originally owed their positions to him, and others whom he controlled through fear. Coercion was most evident in the purges and show trials, which were used to eliminate prominent members of both the left and right opposition from the 1920s. Stalin had not forgotten the old intra-party struggles before he came to power, even though the main protagonists like Zinoviev and Kamenev were political has-beens by 1936.

A minority of Russians continued to defend Stalin's methods after his death. One was his foreign minister, Vyacheslav Molotov. In his memoirs, Molotov accepted that Stalin was harsh and made mistakes. But, as Felix Chuev records, he also said that:

> [Stalin] *alone coped with the tasks then confronting the country … Bear in mind that after the revolution we slashed right and left; we scored victories but tattered enemies of various stripes survived, and as we were faced by the growing danger of fascist aggression, they might have united … It's unlikely those people were spies, but they were definitely linked with foreign intelligence services. The main thing, however, is that at the decisive moment they could not be depended on … Stalin, in my opinion, pursued a correct line: let innocent heads roll, but there will be no wavering during and after the war … The terror was necessary, and it couldn't have been completed without mistakes. The alternative was to carry the internal political debates into the war years* (Chuev, *Molotov Remembers*).

INTERPRETATIONS OF THE TERROR

Historians have ascribed various motives for the Great Terror of the 1930s. Some have emphasised Stalin's personal qualities, which increasingly appeared to verge on mental instability or outright paranoia. Russian historians writing after the discrediting of Stalin's memory in the 1950s have written of Stalin as an aberration, which did not invalidate the legitimacy of socialism as a political force.

This had already been the theme of Trotsky, who was keen to vindicate the memory of Lenin while blackening the reputation of his victorious rival. It is also the interpretation of historians like Isaac Deutscher who were sympathetic to the socialist ideal and critical of Stalinism.

Soviet propaganda rewrites history. Kliment Voroshilov, Molotov, Stalin and NKVD chief Nikolai Yezhov photographed at the Moscow–Volga Canal (opposite). After the purge of Yezhov, the photograph was re-released in a doctored form (below).

Many western historians, and post-Soviet Russian historians also, play down Stalin's idiosyncracies, preferring to see Stalin's methods as a more extreme continuation of those already instituted by Lenin. Some, like Robert Conquest (*The Great Terror*), regarded coercion as inherent in the very nature of Bolshevism. Others see Stalin's brutality as part of a broader Russian tradition of despotic leadership – Stalin was the new Ivan the Terrible or Peter the Great, and communist ideology had little to do with his methods.

There were also more 'rational' explanations of the Terror. The regime needed to create a 'siege mentality' among Russians in order to justify the sacrifices they were asked to make to ensure a success of the economic revolution. There was genuine fear of internal opposition to Stalin's policies given the context of the time. The USSR was surrounded by countries hostile to communist ideology and it was fearful of attack. The regime could not afford to harbour enemies within. There appears to have been a genuine fear either of German influence in Russia or of opposition from the military, which might explain the mass purging of the Red Army officer corps.

The purges could be used to create scapegoats for the difficulties and sometimes the failures that accompanied the industrialisation drive, and once begun, the purges tended to gain their own momentum. The secret police, having begun to deal with suspects and forced to meet its quotas, proceeded apace with arrests without concerning itself too much with the whys or wherefores. Memoirs of victims like Alexander Solzhenitsyn have given graphic accounts of what the victims of the purges went through, and have attempted to get behind the mentality of some of the perpetrators. However, they have had relatively little to say about the cause, because it was difficult to establish a sensible rationale. Fear was often the cause of arrests – for example, Russians afraid of being denounced were often tempted to display their zeal and loyalty by denouncing someone else first. Before his execution, Bukharin wrote to Stalin explaining the atmosphere of distrust which generated more terror: 'This purge encompasses 1) the guilty; 2) persons under suspicion; and 3) persons potentially under suspicion … What serves as a guarantee for all this is the fact that people inescapably talk about each other and in doing so arouse an *everlasting* distrust in each other.'

Another interpretation involves distinguishing between the pre-1934 period and the post-Kirov, post-1934 period. Purges in the earlier period can largely be explained by the regime's knee-jerk reaction to problems caused by radical policies such as collectivisation, which met with major opposition from those affected and evoked old fears among the leadership about the fragility of the regime, which responded with repression. After Kirov's assassination the purges appeared to have a more direct, considered political motivation. There is evidence that Yezhov, the NKVD police chief, was also following his own agenda, as a zealous support of purging. Therefore, the assumption is that not everything was directly approved by the leadership, which either ignored or actively encouraged initiatives from those below.

Most historians accept many of these explanations as having some validity, but there have still been important differences of emphasis. One of the first major western revisionist historians of this period was J. Arch Getty (*Origins of the Great Purges*). Getty argued that the Soviet

A 1935 poster showing Stalin and army chief Voroshilov. The caption reads 'Long live the Red Workers' and Peasants' Army, Loyal Guardians of the Soviet Frontiers'.

ДА ЗДРАВСТВУЕТ РАБОЧЕ-КРЕСТЬЯНСКАЯ КРАСНАЯ АРМИЯ
ВЕРНЫЙ СТРАЖ СОВЕТСКИХ ГРАНИЦ!

government was dictatorial but not totalitarian. He concluded that Stalin was not the all-powerful autocrat, arguing that the regime was not efficient enough to impose its views at will, the administration was subject to incompetence and inertia, and orders from Moscow were not always carried out. He also argued that there was still political infighting among leading Party members – for example, Molotov wanted a more ruthless approach to industrialisation than Grigory Ordzhonikidze, while Andrei Zhdanov wanted more emphasis on propaganda and political education than police chief Yezhov, who favoured repression. Getty concluded that Stalin had no master plan and did not initiate everything, although he sometimes intervened personally in events. According to Getty:

> [The Terror] *was not the result of a petrified bureaucracy stamping out dissent and annihilating old radical revolutionaries. In fact, it may have been just the opposite ... rather a radical, even hysterical, reaction to bureaucracy. The entrenched officeholders were destroyed from above and below in a chaotic wave of voluntarism and revolutionary Puritanism* (Getty, *Origins of the Great Purges*).

A 1933 design for the massive 'Palace of the Soviets'. The construction was never completed.

The radicalism of the 1930s was eventually replaced by a respect for authority only because of the emergency situation created by the 1941–5 war and the problems of running an increasingly complex economy.

Critics of Getty's arguments have pointed out that while Stalin may not have controlled every move, he clearly approved of most of what went on. When he decided in 1939 that the mass purging should cease, it stopped with remarkable rapidity, suggesting that he still pulled the strings when it mattered. Nevertheless, Getty sparked a productive debate leading historians to investigate exactly how monolithic Russian society was and the extent to which ordinary people coped with extraordinary conditions. Sheila Fitzpatrick, for example, concluded that the terror was less traumatic for peasants than the earlier famines had been, and that workers and peasants suffered relatively much less than high status groups.

Access to increasing numbers of contemporary sources has led several historians to suggest that the earlier picture of an intimidated, manipulated population is too one-dimensional. Historians such as Sarah Davies have suggested that:

> The Stalinist propaganda machine failed to extinguish an autonomous current of popular opinion. The machine itself was far from omnipotent, lacking sufficient resources and personnel to make it fully effective. Whole regions and social groups remained excluded from its influence at various times, and the propaganda that it did manage to transmit was sometimes communicated in a distorted form. The propaganda had to compete with a remarkably efficient unofficial parallel network of information and ideas (Davies, *Popular Opinion in Stalin's Russia*).

Ordinary people were more concerned with the struggle for their basic existence than with politics. Negative attitudes to the regime were often expressed in jokes and grumbles, although these did not necessarily mean complete rejection of the regime. The regime itself did take some account of grass roots discontent. This would help to explain, for example, the concessions made to the peasants' desire for some private property in light of their clear hostility to the collectives. But it seems that complete uniformity of this view didn't exist. Later reformers like Khrushchev and Gorbachev grew up in Stalin's USSR and at some stage began to query some of the policies, if not the fundamentals, of Stalinism.

CONCLUSION

There is not enough space to permit a detailed analysis of Soviet society as a whole in the 1930s. The regime used a variety of methods to mobilise support for its policies. Stalin allowed a cult of personality to

An example of Stalinist propaganda, casting the people of Russia in a heroic mould. It was built for the Soviet Pavilion at the 1937 Paris World Exhibition.

develop around himself, in contrast to Lenin, who despised the emphasis on personality, although he could not prevent a cult being created around his memory after his death. This was mainly due to Stalin, who used Lenin's name to give moral authority to his own policies. While Stalin's successor Khrushchev did not develop a personality cult himself, Brezhnev returned to the Stalinist model in the 1970s, although this model itself had similarities with the approach of earlier tsars.

Stalinism was able to take advantage of modern technology such as the cinema, as well as using art and other forms of cultural expression to glorify both leader and regime. A strong feature of Stalinism was the use of culture as a political weapon, although as suggested on page 117, historians debate its effectiveness. There is certainly evidence of increased participation by Soviet citizens in various cultural activities, organised sport and increasing numbers of public celebrations.

What is still open to debate is the extent to which this involvement was voluntary and produced enjoyment and participation for their own sake, and the extent to which the participation was forced. Did it succeed in getting across the political message that underlay all state- and Party-sponsored activities? To what extent did Russians enjoy Socialist Realism for its own sake? Did they appreciate the political agenda that influenced all cultural expression?

There is a common assumption that the emphasis on influencing young minds through education and organisations such as the *Komsomol* (the Communist youth movement) was effective in influencing attitudes among a more susceptible section of the population. However, it is difficult for historians to assess the success of the regime's activities on minds and attitudes as opposed to people's actions.

The so-called 'totalitarian' school of history was influenced very much by the experiences of writers living in the time of both Soviet Russia and Nazi Germany, and also the subsequent Cold War period. It was represented by historians and philosophers such as Hannah Arendt (*The Origins of Totalitarianism*). This school of thought tended to represent the USSR as a totalitarian monolithic state in which the regime controlled all aspects of material existence and opinion.

Partly because of access to more evidence and partly because of the perspective created by the passage of time, historical discussion has become more diverse. Historians like Sheila Fitzpatrick (*Cultural Revolution in Russia 1928–31*) have demonstrated the diversity of opinion inside the USSR.

This diversity ranged from apathetic conformism to radical Party activism by those who supported the regime avidly and pressed for even more radical measures.

In between were careerists who supported policies with as much enthusiasm as was necessary to secure advancement, or citizens who supported the regime not because they were ardent communists but because they were patriotic Russians or believed in the traditional Russian virtues of strong government.

On the fringes were those who probably remained implacably hostile to the regime, at least in their minds if not in action, perhaps because they had suffered from the loss of their farms or because they were languishing in a labour camp.

What is certain is that the history of the 1930s can no longer be referred to simply as 'Stalin's dictatorship'. While Stalin was clearly the supreme leader, he presided over a society more diverse than was allowed for by critics of the time or by the first generation of historians writing after his death.

4 What impact did the war of 1941–5 have on the USSR?

THE GREAT PATRIOTIC WAR

The Great Patriotic War of 1941–5 had a traumatic effect on the USSR, not least psychologically. The USSR suffered so much damage and such loss of life that it influenced the mentality of the population for subsequent generations. It reinforced feelings of insecurity in a hostile world. Yet, ironically, the war also had the effect of strengthening Stalin's position and prestige, and made him an international figure as well as Soviet leader (even though he remained an enigma both inside and outside the USSR).

The USSR had the moral authority of being a leading member of the alliance that defeated Nazi Germany. The war also left the USSR in control of several countries in central and eastern Europe. Communist parties in Poland, the eastern part of Germany, Czechoslovakia, Bulgaria, Hungary, Romania and, for a brief time, Yugoslavia assumed power and instituted their own versions of Stalinism, either with active Soviet backing or the promise of it if required.

Although the war boosted Stalin's reputation, the USSR survived the initial stages with great difficulty, and this had been partly Stalin's responsibility. His devastation of the Red Army officer corps in the purges of the late 1930s robbed the army of experienced leadership and confidence. This was evident in its ponderous performance in the **Winter War of 1939–40** against Finland.

Stalin, who had tried to deflect Nazi aggression by signing a pact with Hitler in August 1939, also refused to accept evidence that the Germans were planning to attack Russia from the summer of 1940 onwards. The Red Army was not allowed to make the necessary preparations to resist the German onslaught when it came in June 1941. Soviet armies on the Russian borders were overwhelmed, with huge losses.

The German armies moved deep into Russia, destroying many of the achievements of the Five Year Plans and threatening the collapse of Stalin's regime. In some areas, such as the Ukraine, the local population initially welcomed the invaders as liberators from harsh communist rule. Fortunately for Stalin, the Nazis conspicuously failed to build on this advantage, blinded by their racial policies and their confidence in victory. Stalin himself had something arguably approaching a nervous breakdown in the initial stages of the attack, although the regime rallied and fought a total war against the Germans from the start.

The German advance on three broad fronts was eventually halted during the winter of 1941. The assault was resumed in the South in 1942, but was finally halted at Stalingrad. From 1943, an increasingly confident Red Army gradually pushed the German invaders back out of Soviet territory, until it invaded Germany itself and captured Berlin in the spring of 1945, ending the most terrible war in Russian history.

HOW DID THE USSR WIN?

Early interpretations of the war experience tended to focus on two main factors. The heroism and tenacity of the Russian people, military and civilian, in standing up to the German onslaught is one main factor. The Soviets utilised traditional Russian advantages – for example, trading space for time as they retreated, and sucking the German army deeper and deeper into Russia, until winter came to the Russians' aid. The second main factor is the various German 'errors' – for example, in making inadequate preparations for a long war, altering the focus of their offensive and delaying the attack on Moscow.

Later interpretations presented more complex interpretations of Soviet success and the impact of the war on the USSR. There was an assessment of the USSR's readiness for war. Some of the problems of the early stages of industrialisation were being tackled after 1937. In particular, some major industrial projects were completed. There were also big unplanned increases in defence spending as the regime became more concerned at the international situation.

On balance it is recognised by most economic historians that economic growth had been resumed by 1941, following a period of stagnation from the late 1930s. It has been widely accepted that the USSR's survival was greatly enhanced, if not ensured, by policies enacted during the Five Year Plans and the early months of the war. Many factories had been built in eastern regions of the USSR, out of range of German forces. Additionally, in 1941 many factories in the West were dismantled and transported eastwards, where they were reassembled to play an important part in the Soviet war effort.

However, this interpretation has been challenged. Victor Kravchenko, an industrial manager at the time, later claimed:

> *A lot of to-do would subsequently be made in the Soviet propaganda about the factories evacuated to Siberia from White Russia and Ukraine. In*

truth only a minor part was removed ... During the period of that pact, Stalin helped Hitler conquer Europe by providing him with ... every conceivable type of material, in accordance with their economic pact. After the invasion, Stalin helped him by leaving him immense riches in military goods and productive capacity and – most shameful of all – tens of millions of people. Failure to prepare will be held against the Stalin regime by history despite the ultimate victory (Kravchenko, *I Chose Freedom: The Personal and Political Life of a Soviet Official*).

STALIN AS WAR LEADER

The Stalinist economic system was well suited to the demands of total war, because unlike other countries it was already centrally planned and used to mobilising labour and materials on a large scale and for specific purposes.

This was not the case in Germany, which did not go over to a total war economy until late 1942. The USSR outproduced Germany from the start, and increasingly so. Once the Germans failed to defeat the USSR quickly, ultimate Soviet success was always likely. Stalin was closely involved in economic planning. Since he was also a key figure in military planning, political leadership and diplomacy, he exercised much more control of the conduct of war than the leaders of any other warring country. In particular, Stalin's command structure proved very effective.

Unlike Germany, where Hitler allowed and even encouraged competing bureaucracies and centres of power, within two days of the German invasion, Stalin had created a unified system of command. This was STAVKA, the Supreme Command, which co-ordinated political, military and economic strategy.

While Stalin was clearly in control, he did give some rein to able individuals such as Molotov in diplomacy, Nikolai Voznesensky in economic planning and Khrushchev in administration. He also appointed key generals like Georgiy Zhukov, who, after the war, praised Stalin's attempts to master the intricacies of military planning after his initial naivety.

Although Stalin made mistakes and was utterly ruthless in approach – for example, having whole national groups deported on the grounds that their loyalty to the USSR might be suspect – he succeeded in galvanising the nation for total war. He did not make the mistake of using communist ideology as a rallying cry. Instead, he appealed to Russia's traditional patriotism. The call was to fight for 'Mother Russia', a call with the widest possible appeal. Even those churches that had been closed were reopened so that Russians could pray for victory.

However, some historians, such as Peter Kenez, have emphasised that German behaviour gave most Russian people little option but to fight for Stalin. Nazi racial policy made the Russians fight on whether they believed in the existing system or not.

The role of the Communist Party in the war has also come under scrutiny. Soviet historians insisted that the Communist Party played the leading role in mobilising and leading the population in the war effort. However, western historians have tended to play down the impact of the Communist Party. There was a rapid turnover in personnel and institutions such as the army were subject to less political interference than before.

CONCLUSION: THE COSTS OF WAR

The differences between the Soviet performance in the two World Wars were impressive. As Mark Harrison has shown (Davies, Harrison and Wheatcroft, *The Economic Transformation of the Soviet Union 1913–1945*), the USSR was able to devote much more of its national resources to war between 1941 and 1945 than between 1914 and 1917.

The country was able to mobilise 10 per cent of the population for military service in the First World War, but 16 per cent in the Second. The defence industry provided 25 times more supplies for each year of the Second World War than the First. Although the impact of the Second World War was far more drastic on the population from the start of the war – the huge numbers of casualties in the siege of Leningrad being the prime example – the privations of war were shared more equally among the population than in the First World War, so that, for example, food distribution was maintained in most instances.

The costs of war were catastrophic for the USSR. Although there is no agreement on precise figures, it is probable that at least one in seven of the pre-war Soviet population – approaching 30 million people – died during the war, a figure just under half the total of war casualties for *all* nations. Some 30 per cent of pre-war capital stock was destroyed. Tens of thousands of villages, factories, collective farms and houses were destroyed.

Many of those citizens who endured the privations of the war years expected a better life when it was all over, but Stalin's priorities were reconstruction, security and the reimposition of Party controls, which had been weakened particularly in areas liberated from enemy occupation.

5 What was the overall impact of Stalin on the development of the USSR?

1945–53: STALIN SUPREME

In earlier parts of this book, there have been discussions of Stalin's role as leader in peace and war and the political, economic and social developments that took place under his leadership before 1945. Apart from his important role in the international politics of the post-war period, which saw the division of Europe into two competing political and economic systems, the beginnings of the Cold War, and significant crises such as the Berlin Blockade and the Korean War, there has been comparatively little research into the last years of Stalin compared with the 1929–45 period. Possibly this is because domestic events in the USSR in the period 1945–53 seemed less dramatic than those of previous years, and there have been fewer differences of interpretation.

Nevertheless, this was a very important period in Soviet history. Whether willingly or not, the events of the war and the prominent, probably decisive, part played by the USSR in bringing about the defeat of Germany thrust Stalin and his country into the forefront of world politics. The USSR was now a major player on the world stage. However, to sustain that role, the USSR had to have a sound economic base. This meant that recovery from the ravages of war was an absolute priority after 1945. To a large extent this was achieved, but it was a relatively short-term victory.

The effort to sustain and increase the USSR's international role put enormous strains on the Soviet economy, and ultimately it could not cope. Although the machinery of the authoritarian state developed by Stalin hid the full extent of this fact from the population at large, and also to a large extent from unfriendly foreign powers, the failure to modernise and adapt the Stalinist economy was the key factor influencing Soviet political and economic development for the next 40 years.

Some of Stalin's successors ignored the problems, and some tried to address them. However, change within the system was difficult to achieve. Communists were not prepared to dismantle the whole structure of political life as they knew it in order to accommodate radical change in other spheres. While not totalitarian according to the criteria of some commentators, the state created by Stalin was sufficiently authoritarian to make meaningful economic change impossible without accompanying political change. However, major political change was inhibited by the fact that the elite had too many vested interests as well as ideological preconceptions to ever tolerate serious tinkering with the political system.

One of Stalin's legacies to his successors was the creation of a fundamentally conservative ethos that was resistant to change, despite the original revolutionary ethos of Marxism-Leninism.

POLITICAL DEVELOPMENTS

Many western historians of the post-1945 USSR have devoted little attention to political life under Stalin. His power seemed even greater and more impregnable than before, if that were possible. The *Politburo* and Central Committee did not meet as full bodies between 1945 and 1952. Stalin seemed as ruthless as ever, as the continuing deportations and 'punishment' of those seen as less than totally loyal during the war showed. Nevertheless, there were still manoeuvrings among the Communist Party elite, particularly by Lavrenti Beria (the feared head of the security services), who had his own enemies.

The general consensus has been that Stalin tolerated this possibly because he felt invincible. After all, the Soviet victory in war had appeared to give even more legitimacy to his regime. But he may also have tolerated it because he knew that, when it suited him, he could exert his own will. For example, Beria's influence began to decline before Stalin's death. Purges continued and although not on the pre-war scale, no one could yet feel safe.

The historical debate about Stalin eventually became less one-dimensional. Some historians, like the post-Soviet Russian Volkogonov, have focused a great deal on Stalin's negative qualities. Other writers from the 'revisionist school' associated originally with Getty have claimed that Stalin was less powerful than often thought, or at least was not responsible for everything negative that happened in the USSR. Some historians, like Walter McCagg (*Stalin Embattled 1943–1948*), have highlighted the supposed power of interest groups such as the managers of industrial enterprises and the army high command. These historians argue that Stalin's associates frequently discussed sensitive issues without feeling personally threatened.

The example that has received most attention is that of Zhdanov, who had been the guardian of ideological purity but was supposedly a 'moderate' in the sense that he supported the idea of continued good relations with the USSR's western allies.

Zhdanov had been widely tipped as Stalin's heir. However, Zhdanov's star was on the wane, and some of his supporters were purged. Defeat for Zhdanov (who died in 1948) does not prove that Stalin's own wishes were successfully challenged, but may be evidence that Stalin, as ever, was prepared to change his stance and his support for particular individuals just as he liked.

After 1945, Stalin made the regime even more insular, reducing contact with foreigners. Some historians, like Peter Kenez, have seen Stalin as all-powerful in the sense that he allowed subordinates to become associated with particular policies, but who would later be demoted if those policies failed. Thus, Stalin avoided taking responsibility for any mistakes.

Kenez believed that the only limitation to Soviet totalitarianism was the fact that it was inefficient (because decisions were made haphazardly), and Stalin became increasingly isolated and given to believing his own propaganda. Nevertheless, historians such as W. Hahn (*Postwar Soviet Politics: The Fall of Zhdanov and the Defeat of Moderation 1946–53*), went much further in claiming that Stalin's power was less complete than is sometimes imagined, with Stalin vying with, for example, the popularity of the Red Army commanders. This would account for Stalin's demotion of the great war hero Marshal Zhukov.

Despite the availability of more archive material, the evidence for Stalin's methods is not conclusive, because there was no open debate, just a lot of manoeuvring behind closed doors.

ECONOMIC AND SOCIAL PROBLEMS

The evidence that is available suggests that the post-war years were extraordinarily difficult for the Soviet people. In the view of some historians like Peter Kenez, this period was even more difficult than the pre-war years or the period of war.

Soviet citizens had been persuaded to believe that their suffering was only temporary and that conditions would improve after victory. But the reality was very different. Demands on the rural economy were actually increased – for example, higher taxes were imposed in 1948 and procurement quotas were arbitrarily varied from region to region as the government saw fit.

Conditions in many rural areas were miserable. Famine returned and, in his memoirs, Khrushchev reported evidence of cannibalism – a feature of previous famines in the early 1920s and early 1930s. The misery was worse in the countryside than the towns. Recovery there was more rapid, because once again the regime made industry the priority, although urban living conditions were probably worse than before the war.

The aim of the fourth Five Year Plan (1946–50) was ambitious: to restore the economy to pre-war levels. The results were impressive, and were achieved by the old combination of hard work, propaganda and coercion, with the addition of materials plundered from defeated Germany. Recovery was probably assisted by the fact that industrial management was more stable. Managers were less likely to be suddenly purged than had been the case in the 1930s.

Economic historians have emphasised that despite the impressive rises in production, and the fact that the Stalinist command economy was efficient from the standpoint of control, in other respects it was inefficient and disruptive, particularly due to the practice of giving priority to certain sectors. However, according to John Keep: 'The defects of centralised planning, which would loom so large in later years, were less evident in the reconstruction period when all attention was focused on achieving a relatively limited number of priority targets' (*Last of the Empires*). The results of the fifth Five Year Plan were less impressive than the Fourth.

In general, most historians regard this period as one of grinding poverty and monotony, with little or no optimism for the future as hopes of liberalisation of the regime were quickly dashed by Stalin:

> *Communist ideology had long been emptied of meaning, reduced to the repetition of meaningless phrases. Professional ideologists … asserted that the country had already 'achieved socialism' and was now building communism. The ideological nakedness of the regime was covered up by the creation of a surrogate ideology of hero worship, which now reached pagan proportions* (Kenez, *A History of the Soviet Union from the Beginning to the End*).

STALIN AND STALINISM

The debate over the extent to which Stalinism was a continuation or perversion of Leninism has been covered briefly in earlier parts of this book. The historical debate about Stalin's impact on the USSR has been heavily influenced by the context in which these interpretations have been put forward.

When Khrushchev and later Soviet politicians and political commentators began to criticise Stalin's 'excesses', they were careful to avoid direct criticism of the Communist Party itself. To have done so would have been to criticise the very basis of the Soviet system and to undermine the legitimacy of the Communist Party to continue in power. It would also have destroyed the credibility of later leaders, who continued, right down to Gorbachev in 1985, to profess their belief in the Communist Party as the leading force in society. In 1987, Gorbachev himself was careful to distinguish between Stalinism and socialism, declaring of Stalin's personality cult that 'it was alien to the nature of socialism, represented a departure from its fundamental principles and, therefore, has no justification'.

However, by focusing the criticisms on Stalin, Russian commentators reinforced the impression, already current in the West, that what was analysed under the heading of 'Stalinism' was synonymous with the man himself. While nobody has denied that Stalin made his own indelible mark on Soviet society, the unanswerable question is: 'Would the USSR have taken a different course of development had a different man been in power?' Historians like Conquest and Pipes doubt it would have done. They believed that the negative features of Stalinism were inherent in Bolshevik ideology, and were already practised to a large extent by Lenin. Many historians believe that a regime led by Trotsky would have been equally as ruthless.

In the context of Russian and Soviet history, the following can be said about Stalin's USSR.

- The concept of the Russian leader as dictator was not new. It was part of Russian tradition, which had no experience of democracy except for a brief period after the February revolution of 1917. Some earlier tsars like Peter the Great had been as ruthless as Stalin in getting their own way, and Lenin was equally ruthless in dealing with those who stood in the way of his regime. If anything was different about Stalin's methods, it was the scale of his ruthlessness, as evident during periods such as collectivisation and the Great Terror. It was also true of his behaviour during and after the Second World War. Coercion was institutionalised on a grand scale. This enabled the regime to exert much greater control over people's lives than had been possible in earlier days. Methods of control became so institutionalised that the instruments of coercion, reinforced by propaganda, could operate independently of the leader. This doesn't mean that we should necessarily accept that Stalin was a 'weak dictator'. On the contrary, right up until his death he would intervene personally – for example, to institute purges – if he thought it desirable.
- Historians have debated the extent to which Stalin became mentally unstable, and whether he thought through his policies rationally. We shall probably never know. Given Stalin's background and the fact that he was not a Russian, he was always something of an outsider. Stalin, like all politicians, used the ideology of his party to justify his actions, and the all-pervasive philosophy of Marxism-Leninism espoused by communists gave them enormous self-confidence. However, we cannot be certain of the exact motivation of Stalin at any given moment.
- 'Stalinism' is a useful concept for analysing the Soviet economy, society and political system during this period, and has been used as such by

many historians. It also has its limitations. There is a danger of over-rigidity of approach. For example, Stalin's foreign policy was never dictated by ideology, despite the conviction of successive western governments during the Cold War. Stalin was obsessed with security for the USSR. This dominated his policy towards central and eastern Europe in the period after the Second World War. There is no convincing evidence that Stalin had any interest in extending Russian power beyond the *cordon santitaire* established in this period, and certainly his policies were not dictated by any belief in Marxist internationalism. Stalin was quite scrupulous in observing some international agreements – for example, by carrying out his promise to the West not to become involved in the Greek Civil War. Stalin's successors showed far more interest than he did in extending Soviet power worldwide, not in terms of physical occupation but in terms of having the military capability to act beyond the borders of Europe. It was Stalin's successors who built up the Soviet navy and tried to compete with the USA in global terms.

- There were changes of emphasis during Stalin's time in power. Clearly, the 1930s saw a more authoritarian approach than the period of NEP Russia, with the state taking a more direct role in moulding culture and enforcing political consensus as well as directly running the economy. Yet there were changes of emphasis even during the 1930s. During the later 1930s there was a growing emphasis on loyalty to the Communist Party and state. In 1939, Stalin emphasised the concept of 'socialist legality' to signify the end of mass terror. During the war, Russian patriotism and anti-fascism were the watchwords. In Stalin's final years there was a renewed campaign against foreign influences in all areas of life, including the arts and sciences. In other words, the regime adapted to the perceived needs of the time. To what extent Stalin led these developments, or went along with those suggested by underlings, has been a matter of debate. However, despite changes in policy the important fact is that the regime was conservative in so far as there could be no questioning, let alone discussion, of the fundamental tenets of the socialist state as perceived by the leadership.

To what extent did Stalin succeed in modernising Russia and making it a substantial economic power? NEP had helped Russia recover from the ravages of revolution and war, but was only a very partial step on the way to creating an industrial or socialist society. The strategies of collectivisation and industrialisation adopted at the end of the 1920s, and closely defined, were intended to rectify this. Stalin adopted the methods of earlier tsars and Witte in increasing taxation and building up both industry and defence, although on a much larger scale.

By the time of Stalin's death the USSR had, as a developing country, completed the first stages of industrialisation. The process had been rapid because an authoritarian government had made this the absolute priority and had taken no account of the human cost involved. During this process, the USSR managed to win a total and devastating war, emerging as a superpower, superficially at least, on a par with the USA. At the same time, there was a massive social transformation. By the 1960s there were 33 million people employed in industry and construction compared with 5 million in 1928. In terms of the original objectives, therefore, there had been considerable successes.

However, there were also failures. In 1917, the communists expected to provide a blueprint for a socialist industrial society for the world, not just Russia. This had conspicuously failed to happen, although the Soviet approach to rapid industrialisation was adopted as a model by some other countries seeking to modernise quickly. The Stalinist economic model proved effective in creating large quantities of material, but never solved the problem of how to sustain economic growth of sufficient quality to meet the needs of a more advanced industrial society. Moreover, agricultural development did not keep pace with industrial development.

Stalin himself appeared to accept that, for all the propaganda about achievement, the problems had not been solved. At the Communist Party Congress of March 1939, he stressed that the USSR still had to make enormous sacrifices and 'further consolidation' if it were to outstrip the capitalist economies. This meant that, although the USSR had constructed socialism, the state could not 'wither away' as had been predicated in orthodox Marxist theory. Rather than move to a society in which citizens administered themselves, the state must actually be strengthened, because the USSR was surrounded by hostile powers.

The function of the state was no longer that of suppressing hostile classes, since these no longer existed. Its function now was to ensure 'peaceful economic organisation and cultural education'. The state had to continue until international capitalism was defeated. Stalin made relatively few theoretical pronouncements after 1945, but there is no evidence that he ever changed this view.

Unsympathetic historians have dismissed the theoretical arguments as meaningless, arguing that Stalin was only interested in preserving his personal power, which was essentially the theme of Russian critics such as Volkogonov.

To some extent, therefore, the USSR had been modernised by the time of Stalin's death. The system had shown it could build up a defensive capability, successfully tested in a brutal war. On the other hand, economic backwardness had been only partially overcome in industry, and certainly not in agriculture. Linked with this last point, self-sufficiency had not been achieved. Central planning, which had been lauded as the triumph of human rationality, had in fact been marked by irrationality and inefficiency. Indeed, one historian, Mark Sandle, called the economic sector 'socialist in form, Stalinist in content' (*A Short History of Soviet Socialism*).

CONCLUSION: STALINISM AND SOCIALISM

Officially socialism had been achieved in the USSR in 1939. The next task was to facilitate the transition to communism. Could this be achieved under Stalin's system? Indeed, what did communism actually mean?

Malia claimed that, in one respect, Stalin had achieved socialism by abolishing some of the central features of capitalism such as private enterprise and other aspects of the market economy. However, what had been traditionally regarded as the 'moral programme' of socialism – features such as individual freedom, equality and freedom from material want – were conspicuously absent, and therefore it was only a partial socialism. Stalin's successors were too much part of the system to accept that socialism had failed to improve the quality of life, but some at least were realistic enough to know that there was a lot further to go before the goal of economic modernisation was achieved.

The dilemma that Stalin's successors like Khrushchev faced was this: could the necessary economic goals be attained without corresponding changes in the political system and the cultural climate? This dilemma was only partially appreciated and only partially addressed in the succeeding years.

PART 3

Post-Stalinist Russia, 1953–85

KEY QUESTIONS

- What changes did Khrushchev make to the Soviet system?
- How successful were Khrushchev's reforms?
- What was the impact of destalinisation?
- Why was Khrushchev removed from power?
- What was Brezhnev's impact on the Soviet system?
- To what extent did Stalinism continue after 1953?
- How significant was Gorbachev's accession to power in 1985?
- To what extent did Gorbachev reform the USSR?
- Why did the Soviet Union break up?
- To what extent had Russia modernised between 1856 and 1985?

THE KHRUSHCHEV ERA

Members of the collective leadership that emerged after Stalin's death in 1953 manoeuvred for power. Individuals such as Nikolai Bulganin, Khrushchev and Georgy Malenkov had their own policies, but the rapid arrest and execution of security chief Beria signified that there was likely to be a modification of Stalin's rigid method of government. Nikita Khrushchev emerged as the leading contender, an impression confirmed by his so-called 'secret speech' to the Twentieth Congress in February 1956. Khrushchev denounced Stalin for errors such as his personality cult and excessive purges. Significantly there was no attack on the Communist Party itself, and so there has been general agreement that although Khrushchev was a reformer, and wanted to make the USSR a more efficient and possibly a more humane society, he certainly had no intention of attacking the monopoly of power enjoyed by the Communist Party.

Some of Khrushchev's reforms came to be known as destalinisation, the dismantling of some of the strict political and cultural controls associated with Stalin. Commentators have debated the success of these measures. They prompted unrest in some Soviet satellites and led to the crushing of the Hungarian rising. There was a brief period of relaxation of censorship. Other reforms had a limited impact, particularly economic and administrative reforms. This was partly due to flaws in the reforms themselves and partly due to opposition to Khrushchev's ideas.

Most historians accept that Khrushchev's eventual fall from power was due to a combination of what were seen as foreign policy failures over China and Cuba, and dislike by the Communist Party of his style and methods.

THE BREZHNEV ERA

It seemed as if the Communist Party was no longer prepared to accept a leader with unchallengeable power as had been possessed by Lenin and Stalin. Leonid Brezhnev, who emerged as leader of the USSR in the late 1960s, amassed great authority and faced no real challenges before his death in 1982. Nevertheless, his power rested on consensus as much as fear. Brezhnev was supported by leading members of the Communist Party because he did not threaten to change the system.

The real issue for debate is the extent to which Brezhnev's USSR was stagnating economically during the period from the mid-1960s to the 1980s, and to what extent the essentials of the political, economic and social system that he inherited were preserved, and at what cost.

GORBACHEV AND THE END OF THE SOVIET UNION

After Brezhnev's death and the leadership of two stop-gap, essentially compromise, candidates in Andropov and Chernenko, a reformer did come to power. Mikhail Gorbachev recognised the need for change if the USSR were to remain an important and stable power in the face particularly of economic and nationalist challenges. His reforms failed, and there has been considerable discussion about the reasons. Was it Gorbachev's own fault? Or was the situation already so hopeless that a reformer who still believed in the primacy of the Communist Party, even a reformed Party, was bound to fail?

Gorbachev was widely hailed around the world as the man who, more than anyone, ended the Cold War and made possible a relatively peaceful transition to post-communism in central and eastern Europe. But he was also regarded, certainly by many in his own country, as the person responsible for the ultimate break-up of the USSR in 1991.

How different was the Russia of the 1980s from the country that Alexander II had inherited? Had the country modernised? If so, at what cost? Could socialism have been implemented in a different way? Indeed, was the USSR ever socialist at all? Could a political system built and maintained by coercion as much as by consent, and with a world view that permitted no rival viewpoint because it was based on a belief in the fundamental inevitability of the historical process, be changed from within to meet the challenges of a changing world?

1 How successful a reformer was Khrushchev?

THE CRISIS OF LEADERSHIP

Although a collective leadership took over the USSR on Stalin's death, tradition and the political structure favoured the emergence of a strong leader. Khrushchev acted promptly in 1953 by taking the lead in the conspiracy to remove Beria, then outmanoeuvred other rivals to acquire the leadership. It has been common to contrast Khrushchev's more open, populist and even more humane style with that of the austere Stalin. However, it should also be emphasised that Khrushchev had risen through the Soviet system by being both efficient and ruthless, as demonstrated in the purges he organised in Ukraine before the war, his organisation of the defence of Stalingrad and his deportation of Jews from Ukraine in the late 1940s. He also showed himself very capable in outmanoeuvring his rivals, although he was helped to some extent by the fact that Stalin had purged most of the other potential leaders before his death. Martin McCauley, like some other historians, considered this a crucial factor in the decline of the USSR as a great power:

> The brilliant Lenin was followed by the crafty Stalin, who killed intellectual debate at the top. Then came Khrushchev, who had only a limited grasp of Marxism. He was followed by Brezhnev, who preferred flattery to hard thinking ... Andropov was never well enough to make an impact. The depths were plumbed by the election of Chernenko. Perhaps one should not be too harsh on him. He could hardly speak. The arrival of Gorbachev was the exception which proved the rule. However, in the end, he destroyed the system. The limited intellectual ability of so many leaders had a catastrophic effect on the way the country was managed. Moreover, the expansion of education had produced many highly talented, educated people in every walk of life. There could not be a debate between leaders and led because the leaders could not prevail in such a debate. The result was a loss of political authority by the leaders (McCauley, The Khrushchev Era 1953–1964).

Although Khrushchev had limited intellectual ability, he recognised the need for reform in key areas of the economy and administration. But he was also realistic enough to follow the existing Soviet practice of promoting his own followers to key positions, although he never enjoyed the authority of earlier leaders – a major factor in his downfall.

ECONOMIC REFORM

Until 1953, there had been no major shifts in economic policy since the introduction of the Stalinist command economy. But there had been important structural changes. For example, by 1953 agriculture was responsible for only one-fifth of the gross national product (GNP) compared with almost half in 1928. The workforce was now better educated and better trained, and it contained many more women. Industrial advances had been one-sided. The biggest advances had been made in some capital goods industries like steel, and in defence equipment. Least advance had been made in the consumer goods industries and in agriculture.

Under Khrushchev, for the first time there was a major shift in economic and social policy. Investment in agriculture increased by 250 per cent between 1953 and 1958, and there was substantial investment in urban housing construction and the production of consumer goods. There was major investment in education and the health services and there was considerable expansion of foreign trade, mostly with the communist states of eastern and central Europe. The results were mixed. Industrial production in the 1950s increased more rapidly than in the USA, because the USSR invested a greater proportion of its wealth in industry, particularly the capital sector. However, because the centralised Stalinist economy was in place, there was considerable waste and inefficiency. Investment in defence increased at almost twice the rate of industrial production as a whole, and took up a higher proportion of GNP than in the USA. This put enormous strain on the poorer Soviet economy. The standard of living improved considerably for the first time since the 1920s – as evident, for example, in the decline in infant mortality.

Furthermore, the rate of growth in agricultural production slowed significantly after 1958. This was due partly to the variable performance of grain output from the Virgin Lands, cultivated for the first time in this period, and partly to a decline in agricultural investment because priority was given to defence and the capital goods industries. Although the volume of foreign trade increased significantly under Khrushchev, it still represented a smaller share of national income than in capitalist economies. Imports of advanced technology were insufficient. Although the USSR achieved great technical feats – notably the launching of the Sputnik satellite in 1957 and the first manned spacecraft in 1961 – technological innovation was weak in the economy as a whole. The economy remained labour intensive and low on productivity.

ADMINISTRATIVE AND STRUCTURAL REFORM

Khrushchev accepted the need for structural changes to overcome the economic difficulties identified on page 136 – hence his scheme for regionalisation of industry in 1957. The Stalinist practice of having individual ministries responsible for particular industries throughout the USSR was replaced by regional economic councils responsible for all industry in a particular region. The intention was that industry would

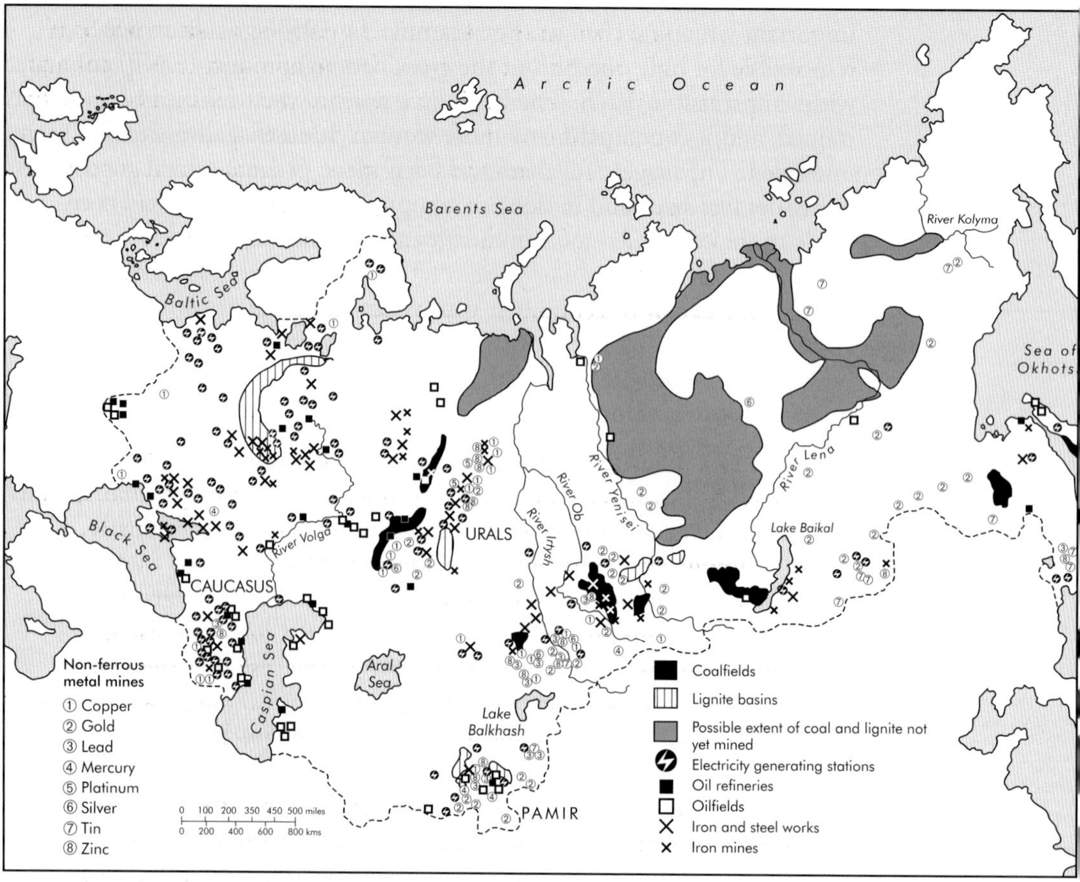
Arctic Ocean
Barents Sea
Baltic Sea
Black Sea
CAUCASUS
Caspian Sea
Aral Sea
River Volga
URALS
River Ob
River Irtysh
River Yenisei
River Lena
Lake Baikal
River Kolyma
Sea of Okhots
Lake Balkhash
PAMIR
Non-ferrous metal mines
① Copper
② Gold
③ Lead
④ Mercury
⑤ Platinum
⑥ Silver
⑦ Tin
⑧ Zinc
0 100 200 350 450 500 miles
0 200 400 600 800 kms
Coalfields
Lignite basins
Possible extent of coal and lignite not yet mined
Electricity generating stations
Oil refineries
Oilfields
Iron and steel works
Iron mines

Main centres of Soviet industry in the 1960s.

become more responsive to regional or local needs and avoid some of the errors of the 1940s – for example, over-investment in coal and under-investment in chemicals. However, historians like Pekka Sutela (*Economic Thought and Economic Reform in the Soviet Union*) have shown that the result was the creation of a complex system of administration that still operated within the centralised planning system. Similarly, attempts to give collective farms more control over their machinery by allowing them to buy equipment from the machine-tractor stations, which were abolished, failed because there was no change in the overall structure of agriculture. Khrushchev's new ministries were abolished soon after his fall from power.

One of Khrushchev's changes did survive him. His political opponents wanted the government to run the economy. He gave the Communist Party a much more prominent role in this area, which it kept until 1988. However, it is generally accepted that the fundamental weakness of the reforms was that they were expected to produce results within the structure of a planned economy. There was no serious consideration given to a market structure, which would have made the economy more responsive to market forces than to the Communist Party's priorities. To do so would have destroyed the Soviet conception of socialism.

Some interest was shown in the Hungarian model of 'market socialism', which allowed state-run firms to respond less to administrative plans and more to perceived market needs. But these ideas were rejected because they were felt to be incompatible with the Soviet political system. Ironically, the Hungarian experiments did influence the next generation of reformers such as Andropov and Gorbachev, although they also encountered the expected resistance from Party die-hards when the experiments were discussed. For the time being under Khrushchev, propaganda helped to disguise the extent of economic weaknesses and failures.

FAILURE

Khrushchev's other reforms, particularly destalinisation, are dealt with on pages 142–5. But he also played a prominent role in foreign affairs, which was very much the preserve of the Communist Party. Additionally, he made an important contribution to Marxist theory on class warfare by announcing the policy of Peaceful Co-existence. This changed the previous official line that violent conflict between the capitalist and communist worlds was inevitable. It was still the case that the two systems would compete for supremacy, but it was no longer accepted that this must involve a catastrophic all-out war in the nuclear age.

This was realism on the part of Khrushchev, but the effect was partly undone by his boasting of the power of Soviet missile weaponry. This boast, although it exaggerated Soviet power, alarmed the USA into increasing its nuclear arsenal and widening the gap between itself and the USSR. The Soviets tried to respond in turn. In the long term, the Soviet attempt to maintain parity with the USA bankrupted the USSR; in the short term, it was one of the reasons that prompted Khrushchev into the Cuban missile affair, which led to an eventual Soviet climb-down. While this climb-down preserved world peace, it was regarded by many of Khrushchev's colleagues as a humiliation. Nor were they impressed with the decline in relations with communist China, which had much less respect for Khrushchev than his predecessor Stalin.

Some interpretations of Khrushchev's Cuban policy regard it as an opportunistic attempt to trade on the friendship of a friendly state to achieve a prestigious foreign policy success and increase Soviet security against the USA. Others have seen a more sophisticated tactic of trying to persuade the Americans into a settlement that would include a resolution of the long-standing impasse over the situation of Berlin. Either way, Khrushchev miscalculated. Not only was he responsible for further increasing US determination and defence spending, but also he gave ammunition to his own critics in the USSR.

Khrushchev's pronouncement in 1962 that the USSR was well on the way to achieving communism and overtaking the standard of living of the advanced capitalist world was absurdly optimistic. Apart from his failures in domestic and foreign policy, he encountered considerable difficulties from within the Communist Party. His reforms of the Communist Party included its reorganisation into industrial and agricultural wings. Regional Party committees found their influence reduced, and Party bureaucrats were no longer guaranteed a post for life.

Khrushchev neglected the interpersonal skills that had once helped him to the top, and hostile Party bureaucrats frustrated his administrative reforms. He simply did not have the power that Stalin had possessed. Although Khrushchev had survived earlier attempts to oust him, he failed to keep the Central Committee packed with his own supporters, a mistake Stalin would never have made. While on holiday in October 1964, he was 'retired' by the Central Committee.

Khrushchev was the only Soviet leader to be ousted by a coup. It was in the Russian tradition that weak or careless leaders did not rule for long. Nevertheless, Khrushchev's dismissal signified an important change in Soviet political practice. The defeated leader was not punished or purged, but allowed to live out his days in retirement, albeit a bitter one.

Martin McCauley has assessed Khrushchev as a 'courageous failure'. He was courageous to the extent that when he took power, he realised immediately that although Stalin's USSR had become a world power, its population was downtrodden and it was not performing well economically. Khrushchev tried to increase productivity, initiative and efficiency, but in his eyes it also meant making the Communist Party more efficient at running the country. Initially, Gorbachev was to try this policy. But he realised too late that he could not rely on the Communist Party to achieve the necessary goals. Khrushchev found this too, because the bureaucrats on whom he relied to administer reforms had gained their positions under Stalin and were not about to remove the essential elements of Stalinism that involved controlling all aspects of life.

According to McCauley, Khrushchev 'chose to reform without using coercion, but this emboldened his opponents to risk opposing him' (*The Khrushchev Era 1953–1964*). There was already a division between conservatives like Molotov and Kaganovich, who thought the economy should be run by central ministries, and innovators like Khrushchev and Malenkov who believed in more managerial autonomy and less central interference. The failure of Khrushchev, due partly to opposition from conservatives, returned the initiative to the centralisers, which was why economic modernisation gave way to stagnation and created yet more problems for Khrushchev's successors: Brezhnev, who largely ignored them, and Gorbachev, who tried to tackle them but was overwhelmed.

Donald Filtzer (*The Khrushchev Era: De-Stalinisation and the Limits of Reform in the USSR, 1953–1964*) emphasised Khrushchev's dilemma in trying to modify the more arbitrary and coercive features of Stalinism and motivate ordinary people without changing a political system in which the Communist Party enjoyed a monopoly of power. Ordinary people still did not have a stake in the system, because they could not elect their rulers, and those rulers resisted Khrushchev's attempts to turn them into selfless reformers. For the time being, the views of Khrushchev's conservative critics prevailed: to tinker with the system was a dangerous exercise that could fatally weaken the whole Soviet system.

CONCLUSION

Khrushchev was like Stalin to the extent that he was a pragmatist. He once declared that 'it was no use everyone having the correct ideology if they had to walk around without any trousers on'. But historians like Geoffrey Hosking (who referred to Khrushchev as 'in some ways an outstanding statesman') and John Keep (who sympathised to some extent with Khrushchev's dilemma), also recognised the very real differences from Stalin. They noted in particular the fact that Khrushchev allied this pragmatism with genuine idealism in that he did want to change people's lives for the better.

Less sympathetic was Peter Kenez, who while crediting Khrushchev with trying to solve problems that were inherent in the regime, also concluded that he could be 'fairly blamed for attempting to introduce reforms that were insufficiently considered and created more trouble than they were worth. Those who accused him of "hare-brained"' schemes were not unjust' (*A History of the Soviet Union from the Beginning to the End*).

Khrushchev was not a liberal, but politicians who progressed through the ranks in Stalin's Russia were not liberals. According to Keep 'the basic fault … lay not in his character but in the system he headed, which set narrow limits on what any leader, however gifted, could achieve' (*Last of the Empires*).

2 What was the extent of destalinisation?

THE ORIGINS

Destalinisation actually began before Khrushchev's 1956 speech to the Communist Party Congress. In 1955, the Central Committee set up a commission to investigate so-called 'abuses of power' by Stalin, and some prisoners were released from the camps. However, the commission emphasised that the Communist Party as a whole was not being investigated, and many of Stalin's policies – including his liquidation of opponents such as 'Trotskyists' and his policies of industrialisation and forced collectivisation – were defended.

This set the tone for Khrushchev's subsequent campaign, which was quite limited in scope within the USSR. The implications were perhaps greater in those countries in central and eastern Europe outside the USSR but under Soviet influence. Those victims of the purges who were posthumously rehabilitated were limited mainly to prominent Communist Party and military victims, and not ordinary citizens. The Party itself was vigorously exonerated from blame.

DESTALINISATION IN PRACTICE

The term 'destalinisation' is misleading because there was never any attempt to dismantle the Stalinist system, or certainly not its principal political and economic planks.

Mark Sandle (*A Short History of Soviet Socialism*) claimed that a more decisive break with the Stalinist past came in the social and cultural sphere, since there were fewer powerful vested interests to oppose change in these areas. Other historians agree that Khrushchev addressed a number of social problems that had been neglected for over 25 years. However, Donald Filtzer argued that for all Khrushchev's ambitious reforms, he brought surprisingly little change to Soviet society (*The Khrushchev Era*).

There were several developments in Khrushchev's USSR following the 1956 Congress speech. Censorship was relaxed, which led to a flowering of literature and other forms of free artistic expression. One of the most famous works published at this time was Solzhenitsyn's *One Day in the Life of Ivan Denisovitch*, an exposé of Stalin's convict empire. The significance of the individual was reasserted. Many prisoners were released. However, Khrushchev himself disapproved of some of the results. Like Lenin before him, he was very much a traditionalist in his cultural tastes. The KGB was reformed and made more accountable to the Communist Party. The ordinary police also lost some privileges. This has sometimes been described as a move back towards socialist legality.

Elitism was attacked, particularly in the higher ranks of the Communist Party. In education, universities were encouraged to take more students from the working class, and there was a greater emphasis put on vocational training in education generally. The reform was badly implemented because too little thought had gone into the resourcing. The educational reforms were so unpopular among the privileged elite that they were reversed after Khrushchev's fall from power.

Destalinisation was not extended to the Church – rather, the opposite. Khrushchev launched a brutal campaign against it, with many churches closed and clergy arrested, presumably because he wished to emphasise his communist, and therefore anti-religious, credentials. In 1957, Khrushchev's enemies in the Presidium, alarmed by the speed and nature of destalinisation, attacked him and tried to secure his resignation. Khrushchev got enough support from the Central Committee to survive this attack, and he responded by sacking several of his opponents, labelled the Anti-Party Group. However, after their dismissal, these individuals were treated humanely and allowed to keep their privileges. Khrushchev tried to make the Communist Party more responsive to the opinions of ordinary members. Structural changes in the Communist Party introduced the principle of rotation of office, a very unpopular move with many Party bureaucrats.

The legal system was reformed. For example, the new criminal code of 1958 required citizens to be charged with specific violations rather than vague offences such as being an 'enemy of the people' or of belonging to a particular social group. 'Comrades' courts' dealing with some minor offences at a very local level proved less popular.

THE IMPACT OUTSIDE THE USSR

Despite the emphasis on denouncing Stalin rather than his followers, destalinisation nevertheless implied that the Communist Party was not infallible. This provoked unforeseen consequences in Soviet-controlled eastern and central Europe, where there was no mass support for communist regimes dependent largely on Soviet backing for their survival.

The Soviet authorities should have been forewarned, since there had been outbreaks of unrest in East Germany and Czechoslovakia after Stalin's death in 1953. The principal outbreaks of discontent in 1956 were as follows.

Strikes and demonstrations in Poland. The Polish communists independently elected a new leader, Wladyslaw Gomulka. The Soviets threatened invasion, but the Poles stood firm, and the USSR backed down. This appeared to signal elsewhere that Moscow would not fight to preserve Stalinism.

Anti-communist demonstrations in Hungary. These became out of hand, and it looked as if Hungary would leave the Warsaw Pact. The Soviets invaded Hungary to crush the rising by force.

Anger in China. Destalinisation also provoked anger in China, where the hard-line communist leadership admired Stalin, but not Khrushchev.

In the longer term, the events of 1956 were an inspiration for later attempts to reform or overturn communist rule, as in **Czechoslovakia** in 1968.

These developments served to emphasise to conservatives in the USSR the dangers of Khrushchev's approach, and were one of the reasons for his eventual removal from power. However, they also signified that, at this stage, the USSR was not prepared to tolerate any breach of its security system in central Europe and would resist a major attempt to overturn communism there.

Some commentators, for example Michael Shafir (in *Khrushchev and Khrushchevism* edited by M. McCauley), argued that 'Khrushchevism' amounted to a legitimisation of different paths to socialism. However, all those paths had to lead to Moscow: there were limits to freedom. Therefore, Khrushchev was prepared to tolerate Gomulka in Poland, because he promised to maintain communist control there. He was not prepared to accept Imre Nagy in Hungary, because Nagy's reforms were too radical and might have led to a multi-party state and the end of the communist monopoly of power. Thus the reform movement in Hungary was crushed.

CONCLUSION

The limitations of Khrushchev's economic reforms were analysed on pages 135–7. The political, social and cultural reforms also had a limited impact, at least in the long term. The fundamentals of the old Stalinist order were still in place, and Khrushchev's fall from grace meant that the

KEY EVENT

Czechoslovakia, 1968 The USSR and its eastern bloc allies invaded Czechoslovakia in August 1968 to crush a major reform movement that threatened to weaken or destroy communist control in Czechoslovakia. Although the action was widely condemned in the West, the *Soviets* secured the removal of the reforming Czechoslovak leader Alexander Dubcek, and restored firm communist control.

conservatives still ruled the roost. There had been some positive developments as far as ordinary citizens were concerned. There had been some improvement in their living conditions.

Most commentators agree that although personal freedoms were still very restricted, the average citizen who conformed could feel more secure. Graeme Gill argued that destalinisation discredited the model of the single all-powerful leader and restored the primacy of the Communist Party. Certainly, Khrushchev tried to revitalise the Communist Party and also involve more citizens in active participation – for example, by developing the representational nature of *soviets* and getting them more involved in running local affairs.

In so doing, this would have weakened the power of the central bureaucracy. But more significantly, historians like Donald Filtzer argued that Khrushchev failed to provide the substantial political and economic incentives that would really have achieved the gains in productivity the economy demanded. Such measures would have had far more impact on the prospects for healthy growth of the USSR than Khrushchev's measures of destalinisation. Important though they seemed at the time, his limited reforms did not break the fundamental mould created by Stalin, and Khrushchev's successors put an immediate block on any further major move towards modernisation in all key areas of Soviet life.

Filtzer concluded that Khrushchev's rivals were probably right in their fears that destalinisation would start a chain of events that would lead to a collapse of the Soviet system. The Communist Party faced an impossible dilemma: 'If left untouched the Soviet system was doomed to limp along in a state of near-perpetual crisis. Yet any meaningful reform would sweep away the system, and its reformers along with it' (Filtzer, *The Khrushchev Era*).

3 Why was the period after Khrushchev a time of stagnation?

BACKGROUND

As was discussed on pages 136–7, Khrushchev's fall from power was engineered by leading colleagues who disapproved of his style and his reforms, not least those intended to shake up the Communist Party. The theme of the next seventeen years was one of caution and 'not rocking the boat'. The result, as most commentators agree, was to actually intensify the underlying problems, particularly economic ones, that had beset the USSR for many years previously.

BREZHNEV AND CONSERVATISM

Although another collective leadership emerged after Khrushchev's fall, his former *protégé*, Leonid Brezhnev, gradually emerged as the front-runner for the dominant position, being appointed First Secretary in October 1964. Alexei Kosygin, who had more reforming credentials, was a significant figure in foreign affairs. But he did not have Brezhnev's base of support in the Communist Party. Brezhnev was popular within the Communist Party as a whole because he was regarded as predictable and moderate. In other words, he would not behave in the dangerously arbitrary way of Stalin, but neither would he get carried away like Khrushchev with reform.

Some historians, for example Pekka Sutela (*Economic Thought and Economic Reform in the Soviet Union*), emphasised that initially after Khrushchev there was not a complete block on reform. Economic reformers were encouraged to put forward their ideas on modernisation. The most influential of these reformers was Professor Evsei Liberman. He had published an article in *Pravda* in 1962, which provoked considerable discussion in subsequent years.

Liberman did not seek to destroy the system of planning, but he did aim to rationalise its implementation. Essentially, his proposals retained the idea of plans being handed down to enterprises from above, but the managers would have more autonomy in implementing the plans. Profitability would be the sole performance criterion (worked out by comparing the ratio of profits to working capital).

There were anomalies in Liberman's ideas, and pricing would still have

KEY TERM

Pravda Founded by Lenin in 1912, *Pravda* ('Truth') became the official newspaper of the Central Committee of the Communist Party, putting across the official party line. It was the leading Soviet newspaper with a circulation of nearly ten million by 1989.

been fixed centrally. Enterprises would still have been subject to demands from above and the plans would be determined by political, rather than economic, criteria. Therefore, the fundamentals of state ownership and central planning would have remained.

Kosygin introduced some economic reforms in 1965. These partially reformed the pricing system and the system of incentives. But, once again, there was no basic change to economic structures or the basic economic goals. Ministers continued to interfere in enterprises. Where managers did show some initiative, they were then discouraged by being given more obligatory targets to reach.

Economic historians like Sutela and Alec Nove (*An Economic History of the USSR*) emphasised the contradictions in economic thinking. After 1965, Brezhnev's regime occasionally tinkered with different models of assessing economic performance and encouraging initiative, but no fundamental reforms were attempted. Brezhnev allowed the essentials of the Stalinist political and economic structure to remain in place, while

'To the church or the registry office?' – a Soviet cartoon showing the conflict between the old and the new in Russian society.

creating the assurance for the population at large (due mainly to Khrushchev's earlier approach) that, provided citizens conformed at least outwardly, they could feel safe and could expect a gradual rise in living standards.

Stability was comforting, but there has been general agreement that by basically sweeping economic problems under the carpet, the Brezhnev regime was storing up trouble for the future. In contrast, Brezhnev's political success was marked by the fact that his colleagues allowed him to amass honours, promote his supporters and eventually develop his own personality cult that at least rivalled that of Stalin. Only when it was clear that he was dying in the early 1980s (he was kept alive to the last possible moment), did colleagues begin to intrigue over the succession, in true communist tradition.

In some senses, Brezhnev appeared at least as powerful as Stalin had been. For example, despite the earlier determination of colleagues not to allow one man ever again to hold several top posts, in 1970 Brezhnev added the title of 'president' to his leadership of the Communist Party. He was allowed to promote his family to high positions. Corruption proliferated.

However, Brezhnev's elevation and exercise of power were based much less on fear than on consensus. This consensus was evident in the way that there was relatively little change in key personnel compared with Stalin's day, particularly in major institutions like the *Politburo* and the Secretariat. The Party leadership was so stable that the average age of the leadership steadily rose along with Brezhnev himself.

DEVELOPED SOCIALISM

The essentials of Stalinism remained in place. Khrushchev's rash promise that the USSR would become a classless, prosperous communist society by 1980 was quietly forgotten. Brezhnev promulgated the safer doctrine of 'developed socialism' in 1971.

In 1977, a new constitution declared the USSR to be a socialist state, in which the Communist Party remained firmly the 'leading and guiding force'. There was no talk of the withering away of the state. Despite the guarantees of human rights, active dissidents like the writers Andrei Sinyavsky and Yuli Daniel were harassed or imprisoned. There is no evidence that the small minority of active dissidents, or groups like Russian Jews who were harassed because they wished to emigrate to Israel, received support or sympathy from the population at large.

Life was difficult for the minority of dissidents. Many were treated as deviants for criticising the official Soviet 'world view', and were incarcerated in mental institutions. However, compared with the scale and thoroughness of Stalin's purges, Brezhnev's authoritarianism seemed almost lightweight in its impact. Solzhenitsyn could not publish his novels in the USSR, and was expelled from the country in 1974. But as long as they refrained from making overtly political statements, Russian cartoonists, authors and film-makers were increasingly able to criticise the regime indirectly – for example, by satirising corruption. This would not have been allowed under Stalin, but was a continuation of the slight thaw in authoritarianism begun by Khrushchev. Russians joked incessantly about Brezhnev, particularly as he grew old and decrepit, but they accepted their lot.

Some western commentators writing at the time, such as David Lane (*Politics and Society in the USSR*), argued that Soviet politics were effective, because interest groups were able to articulate their views, the government was united, and the great majority of the population regarded the decisions and processes of government as legitimate.

ECONOMIC STAGNATION

Conservative as the regime was, it did attempt to develop the economy within strict limits. During the 1960s and 1970s, there were major attempts to access the enormous natural resources of Siberia through developments such as the Baikal–Amur Railway. The tenth and eleventh Five Year Plans of 1976–80 and 1981–5 gave a high priority to developing reserves of resources such as oil, coal and gas.

KEY PLACE

Aral Sea This large sea was diverted to irrigate cotton in Uzbekistan. The sea contracted by one third in the 30 years after 1960, leaving a poisoned area of salt. The sea is estimated to disappear by 2010, leaving desert. The area suffers from high rates of infant mortality, typhoid and hepatitis.

However, economic planning suffered from the old faults. Although there were attempts to develop the economies of more backward regions such as the Asian republics, the planners ignored environmental considerations, with disastrous consequences in areas like the **Aral Sea**. There was still too much inefficient organisation and management. Labour productivity remained as low as before, at roughly half the US rate. The rate of economic growth declined sharply after 1975, and even investment in heavy industry, the staple of the Stalinist economy, declined, largely due to competition for resources from the defence and agricultural sectors.

Defence was a major drain on the Soviet economy. Following the perceived humiliation resulting from the Cuban crisis, the Soviet leadership had taken the decision to make the USSR a world power. This required developing the Soviet navy into a force capable of operating worldwide. It also required massive spending on missile technology to try to match the Americans, and on conventional forces stationed throughout eastern Europe. The USSR did its best to exploit its position as guardian of socialism in eastern Europe by trading with its client states there on terms favourable to itself. Nevertheless, the economic strains were enormous.

CONCLUSION: STORING UP PROBLEMS

To some extent, the underlying problems were hidden from both the Russians and the rest of the world, as they always had been. The West was aware of the best of Soviet defence technology, but the Soviets had always been capable of developing advanced technology in those few sectors to which it gave absolute priority. Advanced weapons systems existed alongside outdated industrial and agricultural machinery. The true situation of the economy was also hidden from the Soviet population. Real wages and social benefits continued to rise gradually. However, there were still shortages of consumer goods, and attempts to improve efficiency, quality and incentives had limited success.

Only a minority of reformists in the Khrushchev mould, particularly among the younger sections of the Communist Party, were not content to 'muddle along'. They believed that the USSR must face up to the economic consequences of attempts to maintain Soviet super power status. The country was stagnating and faced long-term decline. The reformers were in a small minority.

While most historians would argue that the economic decline began before Brezhnev, they would agree with the essence of Peter Kenez's summary of this period:

> The Soviet Union epitomised stability and order, and almost everyone assumed that the regime would continue for several more generations. The very fact that the Soviet system had survived for so long conferred on it a degree of legitimacy ... It was a time when the Soviet Union achieved its greatest international success: it became a world power, second to none. But it was also a time of wasted opportunities, a time when the country's economic decline, now seemingly inevitable, commenced (Kenez, A History of the Soviet Union from the Beginning to the End).

4 Why did the USSR eventually break up?

THE INTERREGNUM BETWEEN BREZHNEV AND GORBACHEV

As Brezhnev was dying, there was a battle behind the scenes for influence in the Communist Party. The designated heir, Konstantin Chernenko, was sidelined by the *Politburo*, which appointed the more reform-minded and intelligent Yuri Andropov as General Secretary.

Andropov was interested in the Hungarian economic experiments of the previous generation, with their greater emphasis on flexibility and initiative. However, he had few answers himself to the USSR's problems. His watchwords were 'discipline' and 'reform' – the former reflecting his previous life as head of the KGB, an experience that made him more knowledgeable about the non-socialist world than many of his colleagues.

Andropov's methods were fairly blunt – for example, instructing the police to round up slackers in the streets, since absenteeism from work was a major factor in low productivity in industry. However, he also gave more initiative to factory managers and linked wages more closely to productivity. Additionally, he was realistic enough to contradict implicitly Brezhnev's false optimism by declaring that the USSR was only at the beginning of the stage of 'developed socialism'.

Andropov was already an ill man when he was appointed in 1982. He died in 1984. He did perform two major services to the state in demoting some Brezhnevite conservatives and promoting a younger generation of reformers like Mikhail Gorbachev. Following Andropov's death, it was widely expected that Gorbachev would become leader. First there was a brief period, probably the result of a compromise agreement, in which the sick nonentity Chernenko, a nominee of the Brezhnevites, served as First Secretary. This period ended with his own death in March 1985, which opened the door for Gorbachev. It was Gorbachev who presided over the last major attempt to reform the Soviet political and economic system. In failing, he also presided over the break-up of the Soviet Union.

WESTERN INTERPRETATIONS OF GORBACHEV'S ACHIEVEMENTS

It is generally accepted that Mikhail Gorbachev achieved the unusual distinction of being far more popular outside the USSR than within it. He was admired in the West for several reasons, and was marked out as a moderniser, although the West overestimated this aspect of his policies.

- Above all, Gorbachev was held to be chiefly responsible for ending the Cold War. He negotiated the first disarmament agreements (as opposed to arms control measures) with the West, signalling even more than Khrushchev that the USSR had a realistic understanding of the world situation. He recognised that a mutual military stand-off with the West was dangerous and ultimately counter-productive. He was the first Soviet leader to argue that in the modern world, the language of confrontation was both redundant and dangerous. It seemed as if, for the first time, the USSR had abandoned the Leninist concept of international struggle or competition being an inevitable and natural extension of the class war into international politics.

- Gorbachev's 'New Thinking' was a positive rejection of the Brezhnev Doctrine. This had justified the intervention of the USSR in the internal affairs of other socialist states (as in Czechoslovakia in 1968), if there was a perceived danger of the communist regimes in those countries being overturned, or of those countries leaving the Soviet controlled defensive alliance, the Warsaw Pact. The importance of this change of attitude should not be underestimated. It was Gorbachev's positive encouragement of reform in central and eastern Europe, and his open refusal to back reactionary communist regimes there that pulled the rug from under these regimes. It was largely responsible for both the overthrow of those regimes in 1989, and the fact that the process (at least outside Romania) was relatively bloodless. Again, this was novel for a Soviet leader. Stalin had exerted an iron hold over central and eastern Europe, and both Khrushchev and Brezhnev had intervened militarily to preserve what they saw as socialist unity.

- Gorbachev was seen in the West as a refreshing change from the old guard. He talked the language of moderation and reform, was seen as statesmanlike and was sometimes regarded as a closet liberal. Ironically, it was these qualities that caused him his greatest difficulties within the USSR, and ultimately made him a widely disliked and despised figure.

Gorbachev and Khrushchev

Although a young leader by Soviet standards when he became General Secretary in 1985, the 55 year-old Gorbachev had served his political apprenticeship within the Stalinist system, although mostly in the post-Stalin period. As an agricultural expert, he was well aware of agriculture as one of the major problem areas in the Soviet economy. However, he accepted the need for change not just in agriculture but in the economy as a whole if the rate of economic decline were to be reversed.

Gorbachev was a mixture of the old and the new in Soviet terms, and historians have debated which of the two, if either, was the dominant feature. His career bears a superficial similarity with Khrushchev in that both were reformers, and both faced considerable opposition. Gorbachev was far better educated and more intelligent, and had had a much more sedate political career than Khrushchev before reaching the top. But just as Khrushchev's schemes were often criticised for being 'hare-brained', so many of Gorbachev's measures seemed poorly thought-out, and he was reacting to events rather than implementing a coherent strategy.

Both faced a fundamental dilemma: they were intelligent enough to realise that all was not well with the USSR, and that some major reforms were needed; but they were also prisoners of the system in so far as they believed in the Communist Party, albeit a reformed one. They were committed to the idea that change should be managed by the Communist Party, which somehow had to earn the genuine respect and support of the population at large. The population would then become full participants in social, economic and political life.

Gorbachev went much further than Khrushchev in one important respect. Khrushchev had relaxed censorship and encouraged discussion of ideas, within limits. Gorbachev believed that if there were to be a really significant change in attitudes, *perestroika*, or reconstruction, must go hand in hand with *glasnost*, or openness. All citizens must have the confidence to discuss alternative ways of doing things. There must be genuine openness and people must take the initiative. This was a demanding expectation, since the Soviet tradition, and to a large extent the Russian one also, had been for the population at large to take orders and respect their rulers. Gorbachev took time to adapt. When the Chernobyl nuclear reactor suffered a meltdown in April 1986, the Soviet media did not admit the fact for several days.

Opposition to Gorbachev and modernisation

In other respects, Gorbachev was a traditional Soviet leader. Like his predecessors, once elected General Secretary he consolidated his position by promoting supporters and demoting opponents. His purge of the Communist Party was drastic in terms of numbers. Between 1986 and 1989, all Republican First Secretaries were replaced and over half of Party officials at district and city level removed. Half of the Central Committee's personnel changed. However, like Khrushchev, Gorbachev was not powerful enough to overcome all opposition within the Communist Party. There were many high-ranking Party members and lower-level bureaucrats who opposed Gorbachev's measures, for the following reasons.

- They feared for their own positions or privileges – particularly since Gorbachev was emphasising the need to expose incompetence and corruption, both of which were rife.
- They had ideological objections to what they saw as a dilution of socialism.
- They feared that *glasnost* in particular would lead to questioning of accepted norms and possibly social instability.

Gorbachev faced not just obstructionism from those in the lower levels of administration, but also apathy from the population at large – to a large extent the product of more than 60 years of them being fed propaganda and told what to do from above. More dangerous in the long run, Gorbachev met disillusionment when reforms were seen to be not working.

ECONOMIC REFORM: 'TOO LITTLE, TOO LATE'

'Too little, too late' was the verdict of some commentators on Gorbachev. His economic reforms were gradual. In 1985, he talked of 'improving the economic mechanism' – that is, making the existing system work better rather than fundamentally restructuring it. Enterprise managers were given more initiative, although they did not always have the will or experience to use it. Crucially, the central planning mechanism was left intact, although the planners were encouraged to interfere less and concentrate on strategic planning and determining priorities for investment. The Five Year Plan was still the chief mechanism. The Twelfth Plan of 1986–90 had the ambitious target of doubling national income by the year 2000. There was actually a move towards more centralisation, with 'super ministries' created for machine building, energy and agriculture.

In 1987, Gorbachev realised that these measure were not radical enough to achieve the desired results. Factory managers were given more say in what to produce and whom to employ. Enterprises went over to 'self-financing', paying for operating costs out of their own profits. Privately owned businesses and co-operatives were permitted, but these rarely succeeded because of bureaucratic obstructionism and popular hostility.

These reforms were unsuccessful. Other reformers like Boris Yeltsin, who was to become Russian President in 1990, criticised Gorbachev for not going far enough. *Perestroika* was based on the assumption that the existing economic system could be made to work more efficiently. Gorbachev would not accept the solution of allowing a transition to a market economy. Years of neglect along with a reluctance to change prevented the Soviet economy from achieving the goals of higher growth and better quality. Ordinary people did not see many more goods in the shops. One Russian listening to Gorbachev talking about *glasnost* enquired, 'What do you eat with it?' There was inflation and a rise in foreign debts.

In 1987, Gorbachev finally concluded that political reform was necessary if economic reform were to bear fruit. Hence the introduction of multi-candidate elections in 1987, although the Communist Party had many

Perestroika in action, 1987. A Soviet satire on pointless bureaucracy.

seats reserved for itself in the new Congress. Although the Communist Party still dominated the Congress – there were actually more Party members in it than before the reform – it was declining in influence, with younger people seeing more possibility of influence in other institutions for the first time since the revolution. Yet, to the last, Gorbachev retained his belief that even with a degree of democratisation in the political system, the Communist Party would succeed in retaining control and therefore the essence of socialism would survive.

More radical steps were finally taken. In May 1990, the Supreme Soviet adopted a five-year staged plan that would lead to the establishment of a regulated market economy. State enterprises would be commercialised, there would be less central interference in prices and the rouble would become a convertible currency. However, economic reform was overtaken by political events.

Decline and fall

Economic reform suddenly seemed irrelevant as the USSR lurched towards dissolution.

- Gorbachev was elected by Congress to a new executive presidency in March 1990. However, he had much less power than any First or General Secretary of the Communist Party had had, and Republican governments increasingly ignored federal decrees. Without the binding force of the Communist Party in control, the Union was already beginning to break up.
- A resurgence of nationalist feeling, both within Russia and the other republics, threatened stability and the Union itself. A draft Union Treaty was approved by referendum in March 1991, but it was a typically unpopular Gorbachev compromise. Gorbachev's idea of a loose confederation with the republics controlling their own internal security and economic resources satisfied neither nationalists seeking independence nor conservatives who wanted to retain the old, Moscow-controlled central structure.
- In August 1991, in a last desperate attempt to salvage the old Soviet system, leading Party conservatives carried out a coup against Gorbachev. The coup was defeated, partly because the plotters themselves were indecisive and had not planned coherently.

'Here is a list of those who don't make home-distilled vodka in our region' – a 1988 satire from Gorbachev's USSR on the black market. Illicit production of alcohol and the resulting alcoholism were major factors in economic stagnation.

'Remember the aim of our attack.' Gorbachev's government battled in vain against major social and economic problems such as drunkenness.

Gorbachev still refused to accept that the Communist Party had had its day. His hand was forced by events as the Supreme Soviet suspended the operations of the Communist Party, and several republics declared their full independence. Gorbachev resigned the presidency and the USSR was transformed into the Commonwealth of Independent States (CIS).

The communist dream seemed dead. The Party had failed, but ordinary citizens also felt confused, uncertain or resentful. Gorbachev later admitted, like Khrushchev before him, that he should have committed himself earlier to more radical reform instead of giving the impression often of reacting to events rather than controlling them. Whether he could have carried out fundamental reform without destroying the political, economic and social order he inherited is debatable.

CONCLUSION: AN INEVITABLE FAILURE?

Most western historians have made balanced assessments of Gorbachev. For example, Martin McCauley is critical of the fact that he 'had difficulty in assessing the consequences of his actions, perhaps his most serious shortcoming'. Nevertheless, Gorbachev eased the transition of a declining power into the post-communist world without a civil war, and without being overly concerned about his personal power.

Despite his failure in many spheres:

> *Gorbachev's lasting legacy is that he led his people out of the kingdom of certainty into the kingdom of uncertainty. They thereby ceased to be prisoners of an inevitable future. Uncertainty then made them free … Gorbachev gave them something precious, the right to think and manage their lives for themselves* (McCauley, *Gorbachev*).

John Keep is more critical, concluding that Gorbachev's miscalculations and failures 'were rooted in a failure to appreciate the true nature of the Soviet political system, which, being totalitarian, was held together ultimately by coercion and mendacious propaganda' (*Last of the Empires*).

According to Richard Sakwa, Gorbachev's legacy was profoundly flawed:

> *By the end, Gorbachev's style achieved the maximum confusion for the minimum advantage … The common judgement at the time was that* perestroika *could only triumph when its exponents had passed from the scene, and this applied particularly to Gorbachev himself … Gorbachev's tragedy was that he was unable to make the transition from party functionary to national leader* (Sakwa, *Russian Politics and Society*).

Peter Kenez regards Gorbachev as being a spent force by 1990. Having tried to return to Lenin's NEP economy of the 1920s, combining what he regarded as the best of socialism with the efficiency of the market, Gorbachev ran out of ideas before the *coup* of 1991. The *coup* failed because the conspirators were as weak as those they sought to overthrow. Gorbachev wanted to protect his reforms, but did not know how to, and actually moved closer to the conservatives by the time of his resignation (*A History of the Soviet Union from the Beginning to the End*).

Mark Sandle is more sympathetic. He concludes that Gorbachev humanised or 'social democratised' Bolshevism (*A Short History of Soviet Socialism*). R.W. Davies (*Soviet History in the Gorbachev Revolution*), writing before Gorbachev's resignation, compares him favourably with Lenin, concluding that Gorbachev's reforms went back to before NEP, to a belief in direct democracy at variance with Lenin's policy of subordinating government to the Communist Party and centralising the Communist Party itself.

Russians were far less sympathetic to Gorbachev, and their judgement was unambiguous. When he stood for election to the Russian presidency in 1996, Gorbachev received only 0.5 per cent of the votes.

5 To what extent had Russia modernised between 1856 and 1985?

BACKGROUND

The collapse of the USSR was unexpected in its speed, both to Russian and outside observers. To some extent this seems strange, since repeatedly during this book there has been a discussion of Russian 'weaknesses' (particularly economic ones) and the failure of various regimes to address them effectively. However, one of the successes of the Soviet regime was its capacity for propaganda to explain why things were better than they seemed, and were getting better. Even western observers were taken in to some extent, and certainly overestimated the strength of the Soviet economy from the 1930s onwards. Yet ultimately it was failure to successfully modernise the economy that caused the break-up of the USSR. The reasons for that failure were complex (as this book has attempted to explain), principally because of the intricate connection in Russia between economic and political concerns.

One of the difficulties of determining the extent to which Russia modernised during this period is the fact that although there were frequent dramatic changes – the introduction of the NEP and Khrushchev's destalinisation to give but two examples – much also stayed the same. Although any chronological division is therefore an oversimplification, the process of modernisation can be divided into tsarist rule (1856–1917), revolutionary Russia (1917–mid-1920s), Stalinism (1929–53) and post-Stalinism (1953 onwards).

Tsarist rule, 1856–1917

Political reforms were limited in scope. No tsar was prepared to see a diminution of his God-given authority to rule his subjects. When Nicholas II was forced to promise political concessions in the 1905 revolution, they were quickly watered down once order had been restored. The *duma* gave a form of representation to the people, but not parliamentary government. Authority was reinforced by the state through the police, censorship (the efficiency and severity of which varied during this period) and reliance on traditional deference to the tsar.

Rule. In the first half of this period, any challenge to the tsar's rule had to be conspiratorial, because of the nature of the authoritarian system. It was also in essence treasonable, because there were no legitimate means of questioning the basis of the regime. Radical political movements such as populism achieved occasional spectacular results, as when key individuals such as Alexander II were assassinated. However, they did not pose a fundamental threat to the regime, because the movements lacked mass support and were undermined by the regime's counter-measures. Opposition groups were also divided between those who looked for inspiration to the West (where some European countries had undergone political transformations), and those who rejected the West and looked to the Russian people themselves for salvation.

Revolution. The 1905 revolution was a serious threat to the regime, but not a co-ordinated one. It arose from a combination of internal unrest with disquiet at a disastrous war. The regime survived what was essentially a series of uncoordinated and largely unconnected events with relative ease once it adopted a strategy of limited concessions combined with repression. The only significant difference in the political life of tsarist Russia by 1914 compared with 1856 was that the later period saw the development of a range of political movements, including non-revolutionary parties such as the Kadets and Octobrists, which sought political reform through the development of Parliamentary rule. Revolutionary parties had achieved little by 1914, despite the attempts of some historians to show a significant growth in political activity at grass roots level. Most of the Bolshevik leaders were in exile in 1914, and Lenin was gloomy about the prospects of real change in his lifetime.

Economic developments. Economically and socially there had been important developments between 1856 and 1914, although historians have argued about their overall significance. Russia still possessed primarily an agricultural economy in 1914. There had been considerable industrial development during this time, deliberately fostered by the state as a means of regaining and reinforcing Russia's status as a world power. However, much of the industrial development was concentrated in relatively few areas, and much was financed by foreign investment in Russia. What modernisation there was created new social forces – particularly the growth of a working class – with which the tsarist state did not feel comfortable. This is one reason why arch-conservatives like Pobedonostev had resisted all substantial reform.

Social and political developments. Socially, there had also been important developments. Serfdom was abolished, but the peasants made few material gains. This is because a rising population put pressure on the land. This, together with often poor quality soil, inefficient small-scale farming and the system of land ownership and organisation, produced low yields. Many of the aristocracy declined in wealth and influence during this period. There was a growing middle class, which wanted more political influence. However, the argument that Russia might have developed more liberal forms of social and economic organisation and made more dramatic economic progress but for involvement in the First World War is very speculative, mainly because of the political climate outlined above.

War. The war itself is generally recognised as the catalyst for revolution. There were many reasons for Russia's relatively poor performance in the war. Political shortcomings and Russia's inability to sustain a major war economically are two of the major ones. In assessing the capability of the regime, comparison with the Second World War should be borne in mind. This war was much more destructive than the First. However, Russia was able to mobilise its resources much more effectively in the Second World War, principally because the regime in power at the time had managed to carry out a major transformation of the economy. It was able to do this because its authoritarian methods enabled it to disregard the human costs involved and to mobilise the population, willing or otherwise, to fight a total war from the start. Having survived the early disasters, partly brought upon itself, Russian victory was assured, proof that Russia *had* recovered and indeed increased its Great Power status.

Revolutionary Russia, 1917–mid-1920s

The Bolsheviks wanted to modernise Russia, both in the sense of creating a modern economy and also in transforming the psychology of the population – in other words, making them socialists. This was to remain the declared aim of subsequent regimes, although the fulfilment of the aim was interrupted by particular events and a conservative ethos that is characteristic of a rigid political system as quickly developed in Russia.

Rule. A desire for change and resistance to change went hand in hand. This had also been a feature of tsarist Russia. The difference was that the pre-1914 rulers believed that the duty to maintain the autocracy was given to them by God. The communists believed that their authority derived from the people. Their feeling of legitimacy derived from Marxism-Leninism interpreted however the leadership of the time decided, but giving it the conviction that it was controlling progress.

- Marxism was a Utopian philosophy that looked to an idyllic future in a classless communist society.
- Bolsheviks welcomed the modern world, and eagerly embraced new technologies and radical social ideas as part of a rejection of the past.
- Socialism was an important stage on the road to communism. And socialism depended on the dictatorship of the proletariat, which depended in turn on an industrial modern society.

However, this bore little relation to the realities of 1917. As historians have pointed out, Marxism was an analysis of nineteenth-century western European capitalism, above all as it had developed in England. It bore little relation to the Russian situation, and Marxists believed that socialist revolution would occur in an industrial society where the proletariat was much larger than in Russia. When Marx considered the future, he was not writing a scientific analysis, but making Messianic predictions about the creation of a dictatorship of the proletariat followed first by socialism and then the communist Utopia. There was no blueprint to follow.

This was even more the case with Lenin. For all his theoretical outpourings and arguments with exponents of other ideas like reformism, Lenin was a man of action, who focused his attention on trying to seize power. Whatever course of action he adopted, he then adapted theory to justify the policy. The NEP was a prime example.

Revolution. Modernisation was the last thing on the mind of most Bolsheviks in 1917. Their coup, the success of which surprised themselves as well as their opponents, led to a crisis situation that involved them in fighting for survival, although a cultural and social revolution went on at the same time. The 'policies' of War Communism and the NEP were not concerned with modernisation but survival against domestic and foreign enemies. Later, however, Lenin justified the NEP as a half-way house on the way to socialism. Other Marxist assumptions, including a conviction that a Socialist revolution could not survive in one country alone, were gradually set aside although never formally abandoned.

SOCIO-ECONOMIC IMPERATIVE?

Economic developments. Some communists became keen advocates of the mixed economy of the early 1920s. Others opposed the NEP. They were uneasy at its contradictions. For example, the communists wanted the peasants to be successful because they needed food. But successful peasants became capitalists and class enemies. Some communists argued that, if anything, by compromising with capitalism, the Communist Party had returned Russia to its pre-1914 state. This was partly true economically, although in the 1920s the state did own the 'commanding heights' of the economy.

Social and political developments. There were more radical changes in political and social life. The years after the revolution saw the firm establishment of a one-party state, employing propaganda and coercion on a major scale. The development of new cultural forms suggested a 'modernising' approach. However, there was recognition within the Communist Party that industrialisation and socialism were still the aims, and most of the ideological arguments of the 1920s were about these aims, although 'socialism in one country' was also about strengthening Russia economically and militarily in a hostile world.

Stalinism, 1929–53: socialism in one country

Stalin's victory in the leadership struggle opened the way for a new economic offensive. It also eliminated doubts and contradictions of NEP Russia. There was no longer confusion about the role of peasants or the proletariat. The former would provide the fodder for industrialisation and the proletariat would carry out industrialisation, inspired and led by the young idealists of the Communist Party. There was no longer room for doubt or complacency. By the mid-1930s the essentials of the economic system for the next 50 years were in place. *SOCIO-ECONOMIC*

- The essence was state control of industry and agriculture. Although state farms represented a small proportion of output compared with collectives, the system of compulsory deliveries by the collectives to the state at fixed prices ensured state control of rural areas.
- Industrial production and investment were physically controlled through a system of fixed prices, planned targets and centrally allocated resources. Elements of this had been present under War Communism, although in a less organised way. Although state intervention in the economy had been a feature of the tsarist economy, particularly under Witte and Stolypin, it had not previously been closely planned.
- Unofficial arrangements (including illegal ones), involving bargaining and exchanges of materials between state enterprises helped to make the central plans work, although not efficiently.
- The economy was still based on money and retained other market features. For example, peasants were able to cultivate private plots, collective farms were able to sell their surplus produce on the free market (compensating for low prices set by the state for quotas), and after the war there was free movement of labour for industrial workers.
- The 'black economy' was an important part of everyday life.
- As seen in earlier parts of this book, the results in terms of industrial growth were impressive, although much less so in agricultural growth. These developments were accompanied by increased Party influence, control and terror. Historians have argued about how systematic the terror actually was, but its scale is universally recognised.

There was early recognition that socialism did not mean a moneyless economy (that would come under communism), contradicting the philosophy of an earlier communist generation after 1917. Therefore the regime was prepared to proclaim that socialism had already been achieved.

The Stalinist system achieved several successes. It ensured a major allocation of resources to investment in capital goods and defence, often achieving considerable economies of scale. However, if the planners got it wrong, the mistakes had a national impact (for example, the USSR did not invest enough in the chemical industry). The system also had another major fault: quality was less of a priority than quantity. Detailed planning discouraged initiative. However, if the planning wasn't precise, enterprises would be encouraged to meet quotas by producing what was easiest to produce, rather than what might actually be needed or wanted. Nevertheless, the system was strong enough to survive the ravages of a devastating war between 1941 and 1945. Ironically, the USSR emerged from the war in one sense even stronger than before, since it now controlled the destiny of a large part of Europe and was recognisably one of the world's Great Powers – although its economy was also severely weakened. Consequently, the post-war years saw an emphasis on economic reconstruction as well as the re-establishment of political controls.

For all its brutality, the Stalinist period was also the period during which the USSR was most confident. The goals were clear, even if Russian nationalism now seemed more important than Marxism or world revolution. As analysts like R. Daniels point out (*The Nature of Communism*), the ideological emphasis of the regime changed. In its early days there had been a genuine, almost religious belief by many communists in the ideology of socialism. Under Stalin and his successors there was a requirement to profess a continuing belief in Marxism-Leninism. But the pragmatic self-interest of the careerist rather than political idealism increasingly drove bureaucrats. Nevertheless, victory in war, albeit at enormous cost which the Soviet people were never allowed to forget, seemed the ultimate vindication of Stalinism, although the population was exhausted and the authoritarian nature of Stalinism stifled initiative and independent thought. INDIVIDUAL + WAR

Post-Stalinism 1953 onwards: stagnation, reform and collapse

As outlined on pages 127–9, the essence of Stalinism survived long after Stalin.

Rule. Although the authoritarianism of the Communist Party and state was less arbitrary after 1953, the essence of the one-party state remained. Politicians were divided broadly into two categories. Reformers like Khrushchev and Gorbachev recognised that some features of Stalinism had too negative an effect on the population. They tried to reform the economy and political system within limits, keeping the Communist Party in control and the ideal of socialism intact. Conservatives like Brezhnev tried to cover over the cracks.

POLITICAL

NO CHANGE

SOCIO-ECONOMIC

Economic developments. Many Soviet politicians and economists recognised that while planning from above had brought great advantages, it discouraged innovation from below. Therefore, under Khrushchev there were attempts to decentralise the economic system within limits, but always under the overall umbrella of the plan. The market sector was not expanded, because it was widely accepted that this would not be compatible with the political system. Because the USSR remained a superpower, and apparently much more powerful in relation to most other powers compared with the Russia of tsarist days, the growing economic problems were underestimated. The economy was in severe need of modernisation. The command economy had been efficient at providing steel in the 1930s, but could not cope with the modern high-technical needs of the later twentieth century.

However, the obstacles to radical change were as great as in the nineteenth century, not least because there was no consensus either on the need for fundamental reform or what form changes should take. This was serious, since the USSR faced new challenges. The capitalist world, led by the USA, showed much more inherent strength than in the recession-dominated early 1930s, and wealth supported expensive modernisation of US military forces. Brezhnev's regime tried to counter this military competition with its own military expansion, but the Soviet economy could not sustain this.

The Soviet regime was in a dangerous situation. Marxists had always based their claim to legitimacy on their assertion that the socialist state stood for progress, particularly material progress, and that it would also transform human psychology. This justified short-term harsh methods, but the promised successes did not materialise, for all the propaganda. Leaders like Khrushchev and Brezhnev were keen to pronounce that the Soviet economy was catching up with, or had already overtaken, the West. They expected the USSR to be the model for other developing countries. The evident failure of the USSR to achieve anything like material parity with the West ultimately proved its downfall. This was because in the modern world, even an authoritarian society like the USSR could not hide the fact from its population – particularly since economic self-sufficiency, which had seemed a reasonable prospect in the 1930s, was clearly not a viable option two generations further on.

Whatever the demands of political ideology and national pride, the USSR could not hope to compete in the modern world without more international involvement and modernisation. The Soviet Union by the 1980s had moved a considerable distance from tsarist days in that it now had a medium developed economy by world standards, with an educated population. In 1917, the tsarist economy had shown it could not cope with the demands of a major war, principally because its industrial base was too small and its communications too primitive. Structural reforms had strengthened some aspects of the economy, although involvement in the Cold War created its own drain on resources.

Gorbachev understood the problem, but did not have the capacity to put things right, despite his initial determination to rectify the situation with the Communist Party still in control. How could he persuade ordinary people to play a bigger role in the economy and life generally without telling them the truth about what was wrong with the existing system? Surely then the Communist Party would lose all its moral authority?

Some historians, like John Keep (*Last of the Empires*), believed the Stalinist system was so faulty that a fundamental reform carried out from above could never have been successful. At least Gorbachev tried to face up to the problems, even if he could not solve them. A more weak-willed or conservative leader might have resisted reform and the Soviet Union might have limped on as a declining power for several years, possibly drifting into a major crisis. At least when the break-up of the union came a short time into Gorbachev's period of rule, it was relatively decisive but peaceful, apart from disturbances in some of the republics. These disturbances were the result of a nationalism that had not been a major problem in tsarist days outside Poland.

The break-up of the Union. The speed of these developments came as a surprise, much as the revolution of 1917 had been, despite the signs of discontent. The collapse created a situation similar to 1917, in that the population was confused and with no obvious model to follow. Both tsarism and communism were seen to have failed. This was evident to all except a few hard-line Party ideologues or those consumed by nostalgia for the past. Many were not optimistic for the future, although the situation in 1991 was remarkably different in one respect from 1917: in 1991 there was a lot of implicit support in the rest of the world for the USSR and a hope in the West that democracy might begin to take root, whereas in 1917 the Bolsheviks had faced a largely hostile world.

What historians have yet to agree on are the reasons for the failure of the old USSR to modernise. Was this because of the impossibility in an authoritarian state of socialism built on the Stalinist model ever being transformed into market socialism or a market economy without fatally undermining the political structure? Or was it because of fundamental weaknesses in leadership; a one-party state does not encourage innovation or free debate, and any disagreement with the official view can easily become identified with dangerous dissent. The leadership therefore failed to give enough people a sense of having a genuine stake in the system, as many had also felt in tsarist Russia.

CONCLUSION

The Russian people faced an uncertain future as the USSR broke up. They were much more free than they had been in tsarist days or indeed in Soviet times, although the uncertainty caused many to look back on the past with nostalgia. The Russian people were still in the midst of an unfinished revolution. They no longer had one pervasive ideology to explain their present or point the way to the future, and yet for the first time since the brief period between revolutions in 1917 they had the opportunity to influence their destinies without undue interference from above. It was a challenge that was both exciting but also frightening for many to contemplate.

A2 ASSESSMENT

As will be evident from reading this book, the main trends in Russian and Soviet history between 1856 and 1985 are clear.

- The tsarist regime was overthrown by revolution in 1917.
- The communists came to power. They established themselves with difficulty. Then they tried to establish a form of socialism in the USSR.
- They survived a total war, but faced increasing problems in attempting to modernise and maintain the USSR's status as a world power.
- Ultimately the attempt failed, and the USSR broke up.

INTERPRETATIONS

There have been several interpretations regarding the significance of particular events, their causes and consequences – both in the short and the long term. Historians do not write in splendid isolation. They are influenced by the events about which they are writing, particularly if the have lived through them, as many of the historians referred to in this book have done. Interpretations have been influenced, for example, by the experiences of the Cold War.

Perspective is sometimes difficult. Historians are still trying to get to grips with the causes and implications of the break-up of the USSR, because it is part of recent history. Interpretations also change because new evidence about the events is periodically unearthed. For example, interpretations of Lenin's personal role after 1917 have undoubtedly been influenced by the release of extensive documentation since the late 1980s, which suggests a more direct involvement by Lenin in the Red Terror than was once thought. Russian historians since the mid-1980s have no longer been subject to the ideological restraints under which they operated before this period.

All this means that although the facts may be clear (although this is not always the case in Soviet history), students will encounter different interpretations. Repeating the names of historians will not gain students extra credit in examinations or coursework. However, an awareness of some of these interpretations and how they contribute to our developing understanding of Soviet history will not only make the history more challenging and interesting, but also improve the quality of students' answers if the interpretations are used sensibly.

EVALUATING EVIDENCE

Students are frequently asked to evaluate a range of historical sources. Whether they are primary or secondary sources is not particularly important in itself. What is important is that students should not make stock responses to source-based questions. A statement such as 'all evidence is biased or subjective' may be true, but will earn no credit unless the content and context of that particular piece of evidence are analysed and evaluated in context.

There is standard advice on how to deal with sources questions in examinations. For example, students should use the mark allocation of examination questions as a rough guide to the length of answer required, whether it be a short answer of a few lines or a mini-essay.

There are always basic questions that can be asked of a source. Who produced it, for whom, when, with what purpose, with what effect? At A2 level, students are unlikely to be asked basic comprehension questions, but they may be asked to evaluate the reliability, usefulness and limitations of particular sources. Reliability and usefulness are not the same thing: a source that is 'unreliable' in terms of authenticity may be very useful in telling us about attitudes – particularly when assessing Soviet propaganda.

Students may also be expected to synthesise information from sources, along with using own knowledge, in answering more substantial questions. The 'own knowledge' element is particularly important in the quest to acquire good marks.

Different examination boards set different types of questions. Some questions will require issues of historical interpretation to be specifically addressed. Others will not require this. However, wherever it is possible to use different interpretations meaningfully in answering particular questions, students will earn credit.

WRITING LONGER ANSWERS AS RESPONSES TO SOURCE-BASED QUESTIONS OR ESSAYS

Whatever the type of essay-style question, a good answer to it is likely to display certain characteristics. A good answer is always one that is relevant, answering the particular question set, and is not a prepared answer. A good answer may well also demonstrate some evidence of reading around the subject and using supporting evidence to back up arguments.

Students are not expected to know the arguments of all historical writers, particularly the most recent, but students should understand some of the different perspectives. It is more important to understand the actual arguments than use the labels. Terms such as 'liberal view' or 'revisionist view' are convenient labels, but meaningless in themselves.

Quotations are useful if short and relevant, and make a particular point. The extent to which students should give their own opinions is always a controversial issue. There may be an expectation that students should state clearly whether they agree or disagree with particular perspectives or interpretations, and assess their value. If this is stated, then students should express their opinion. The important point to remember is that value judgements should be supported by evidence, and not be just assertions.

Relating historians to their wider context and their known philosophical views is also important. Some questions may ask for a particular judgement (for example, 'To what extent do you agree with the judgement that the Bolshevik victory in the civil war was due less to their own strengths and more to the weaknesses of their opponents?'). In such cases there is no obligation to take a particular side. It is equally permissible to write a 'balanced' response, considering the arguments on both sides, or come down more specifically in favour of one interpretation as opposed to another. The important point is that whatever the approach, the answer should not be a series of unsupported assertions, but a considered response that is backed up by evidence.

SAMPLE QUESTIONS WITH EXAMINER'S COMMENTS

Source A
The troubles that have broken out in villages fill Our heart with deep sorrow. But violence and crime do not help the peasant and bring sorrow and misery to the country. We have therefore decided:

… to discontinue altogether after 1 January 1907, payments due from peasants for land which before emancipation belonged to large landowners, the State or the Crown.

> From the Manifesto to better the conditions of the peasant population issued by Tsar Nicholas II on 3 November 1905.

Source B
The Stalinist leadership carried out a frontal attack on the way of life of the peasantry. Collectivisation created havoc in agriculture. Many of the changes brought about by collectivisation were bound to occur eventually in any case. Industrial growth, and with it urbanisation, was likely to accelerate. Collectivisation, however, made the changes extraordinarily rapid and traumatic. The ills of Soviet agriculture, from which the country would not recover for decades, were the consequences of collectivisation. Mass murder for vaguely defined political goals became a possibility – this was the most important legacy of collectivisation.

> Adapted from P. Kenez, *A History of the Soviet Union from the Beginning to the End*, 1999.

Source C
The collective farm completely fulfils the task of further developing the productive forces in the rural areas and makes it possible to harmonise the interests of the collective farmers with those of society and all the people. Living standards of collective farmers have risen tremendously, and the differences in material, cultural and everyday conditions between urban and rural life are being overcome to a growing degree. The socialist transformation of agriculture enhanced the gains of the October revolution, and placed this hitherto most

backward branch on a new socialist path of development. On the basis of Lenin's co-operative plan, the age-long peasant question has been genuinely solved.

Adapted from *A Dictionary of Political Economy*, published in Moscow, 1981.

Questions

1 Study Source A and use your own knowledge. Explain what is meant by 'payments due from peasants for land which before emancipation belonged to large landowners, the State or the Crown' in relation to long-term problems of agriculture in Russia. (5)

Examiner's comments

This type of question is testing the ability to select and deploy historical knowledge accurately, and the student's understanding of the concept of emancipation. Even if the student is unfamiliar with the wording of the source, he or she should be acquainted with the concept of emancipation in the context of the Russian peasantry.

A level 1 answer would do little more than give a basic definition and possibly a very limited description of what the redemption payments were, or why they were a grievance.

A level 2 answer would show a developed understanding drawn probably either from the source or from the student's own knowledge – for example, showing why redemption payments were a grievance going back to 1861, possibly as a concession to landowners which had prevented the expectations of peasants of emancipation being fulfilled.

A level 3 answer would use both the source and the student's own knowledge to place the issue of redemption payments in the context of long-term problems and the protests that were part of the 1905 revolution and that led to the ending of the payments as a concession.

However, the explanation should be brief, in the form of a summary, probably of no more than one paragraph, since only a maximum of 5 marks is available for this question.

2 Compare Sources B and C and use your own knowledge. Comment on the usefulness of Source B in comparison with Source C as an account of the aims and effects of the policy of collectivisation in the USSR. (10)

Examiner's comments

This question is testing not only the ability to select and deploy historical knowledge accurately, but also the ability to interpret and evaluate source material.

A level 1 answer would identify simple statements from the sources or make sweeping general assertions about collectivisation without specific evidence.

A level 2 answer will demonstrate explicit understanding of the usefulness of the sources, bringing some of the student's own knowledge to bear. It may be that there is a focus on 'value by content' – that is, the concept of usefulness is discussed principally in terms of he descriptive information contained within the sources.

A level 3 answer will draw conclusions about usefulness in relation to the issues of the aims and effects of collectivisation. It will note not only the content of the sources but also the context. Source B says more about the effects – which are described as ruinous – although the comments about Stalin's 'frontal attack' on the peasantry implies a very forceful political or economic aim. Source C is clearly an 'official' Soviet source from the Brezhnev era and presents a much more positive interpretation of collectivisation. Answers will probably note the different contexts: one extract is by a western historian, writing after the break-up of the USSR and with perspective; one was written under the constraints of the Soviet political system and contains a strong element of propaganda. Candidates should also use their own knowledge to assess the quality of information provided, considering the various causes and consequences of collectivisation.

A level 4 answer will show a sustained judgement, giving due weight to the content of both sources in addition to using the student's own knowledge effectively.

> 3 Using these three sources and your own knowledge, assess the extent to which the traditional problems of Russian agriculture in the late nineteenth century continued to exist 100 years later, despite the changing policies of the tsarist regime and of Stalin and his successors. (15)

Examiner's comments
This question tests the same objectives as question 2, but it is a synoptic question that focuses specifically on issues of continuity and change in Soviet agriculture.

Students are being asked to do several things, and with 15 marks available, the answer is likely to be a mini essay. The answer should define what the 'traditional problems' of Soviet agriculture were – inefficient farming, poor yields, resentment at paying redemption dues and so on. Then there is an expectation that students will consider to what extent these problems continued, were added to or alleviated. A wide-ranging answer will consider Stolypin's agrarian reforms, the treatment of agriculture under War Communism and the NEP, the 'kulak problem', the aims and results of collectivisation, the concessions made to the peasantry over private plots, the attitudes of the peasants towards the collectives, the imbalance between rural and urban life, and the attempts at agrarian reform particularly under Khrushchev and Brezhnev.

A considered judgement is likely to be on the lines that the basic problems remained the same. These were inefficient farming and negative attitudes by many peasants, who throughout this period resented the fact that they did not own their land (except for the period between 1917 and 1929), were subject to periodic demands from the Soviet state to supply food, and were increasingly under Party control.

High-scoring answers will be those that use both the sources and students' own knowledge, give due weight to key events and themes throughout the whole period, and will probably provide a balanced and supported judgement. A good answer may well address some of the different interpretations, such as those evident in Sources B and C.

SELECT BIBLIOGRAPHY

E. Acton, *Rethinking the Russian Revolution* (Edward Arnold, 1990)

J. Barber and M. Harrison, *The Soviet Home Front 1941–1945* (Longman, 1991)

V. Brovkin, *Russia After Lenin* (Routledge, 1998)

E. Carr, *The Russian Revolution from Lenin to Stalin* (Macmillan, 1979)

R. Conquest, *The Great Terror* (Pelican Books, 1971)

R. Davies, *History in the Gorbachev Revolution* (Macmillan, 1989)

R. Davies, *Soviet Economic Development From Lenin to Khrushchev* (CUP, 1998)

R.W. Davis, M. Harrison and S.G. Wheatcroft, *The Economic Transformation of the Soviet Union 1913–1945* (CUP, 1994)

M. Falkus, *The Industrialisation of Russia 1700–1914* (Macmillan Education, 1972).

O. Figes, *A People's Tragedy: the Russian Revolution 1891–1924* (Jonathan Cape, 1996)

D. Filtzer, *The Khrushchev Era: De-Stalinisation and the Limits of Reform in the USSR, 1953–1964* (Macmillan, 1993)

S. Fitzpatrick, *The Russian Revolution 1917–1932* (OUP, 1982)

J. Getty, *Origins of the Great Purges* (CUP, 1985)

G. Gill, *Stalinism* (Macmillan, 1990)

N. Harding, *Leninism* (Macmillan, 1996)

G. Hosking, *A History of the Soviet Union* (Fontana, 1990)

G. Hosking, *Russia, People and Empire 1552–1917* (Fontana Press, 1998)

J. Hutchinson, *Late Imperial Russia 1890–1917* (Longman, 1999)

J. Keep, *Last of the Empires* (OUP, 1995)

P. Kenez, *A History of the Soviet Union from the Beginning to the End* (CUP, 1999)

J. Laver, *Lenin: Liberator or Oppressor?* (Hodder and Stoughton, 1994)

J. Laver, *Joseph Stalin: From Revolutionary to Despot* (Hodder and Stoughton, 1993)

J. Laver, *Stagnation and Reform: the USSR 1964–91* (Hodder and Stoughton, 1997)

M. Lynch, *Stalin and Khrushchev: the USSR, 1924–64* (Hodder and Stoughton, 1990)

E. Mawdsley, *The Russian Civil War* (Allen & Unwin, 1987)

M. McCauley, *Gorbachev* (Longman, 1998)

M. McCauley, *The Khrushchev Era 1953–1964* (Longman, 1995)

M. McCauley (ed.), *The Soviet Union Under Gorbachev* (Macmillan, 1987)

W. Mosse, *Alexander II and the Modernisation of Russia* (IB Tauris, 1992)

A. Nove, *An Economic History of the USSR*, 3rd edn (Penguin, 1990)

D. Offord, *Nineteenth-Century Russia: Opposition to Autocracy* (Longman, 1999)

S. Phillips, *Lenin and the Russian Revolution* (Heinemann, 2000)

S. Phillips, *Stalinist Russia* (Heinemann, 2000)

R. Pipes, *Russia Under the Bolshevik Regime* (Vintage Books, 1995)

R. Pipes, *Russia Under the Old Regime* (Weidenfeld and Nicolson, 1974)

C. Read, *From Tsar To Soviets* (UCL Press, 1996)

H. Rogger, *Russia in the Age of Modernisation and Revolution 1881–1917* (Longman, 1983)

R. Service, *A History of Twentieth Century Russia* (Penguin, 1997)

R. Service, *Lenin: A Political Life* three volumes (Macmillan, 1991–5)

Hugh Seton-Watson, *The Decline of Imperial Russia* (Methuen, 1952)

R. Sherman, *Russia, 1815–81* (Hodder & Stoughton, 1991)

R. Stites, *Russian Popular Culture: Entertainment and Society Since 1900* (CUP, 1992)

G. Swain, *Russia's Civil War* (Tempus, 2000)

D. Volkogonov, *Lenin: A New Biography* (The Free Press, 1994)

D. Volkogonov, *Stalin: Triumph and Tragedy* (Harper Collins, 1996)

D. Volkogonov, *The Rise and Fall of the Soviet Empire* (Harper Collins, 1998)

P. Waldron, *The End of Imperial Russia, 1855–1917* (St Martin's Press, 1997)

C. Ward, *Stalin's Russia* (Edward Arnold, 1993)

A. Woods, *Bolshevism: The Road To Revolution* (Wellred Publications, 1999)

INDEX